CONFERENCE IN A BOOK™

presents

CONNECT

LEAD

SUCCEED

ESSENTIAL STRATEGIES FOR LEADERSHIP, NETWORKING & THRIVING IN THE DIGITAL AGE

VSA INTERNATIONAL
Virtual Speakers Association

This book is produced as a joint initiative with the Virtual Speakers Association International. All the authors are members of that association, which is a subsidiary of the Global Speakers Federation.

If you would like to know more about the VSAI, its members or events, please visit: *www.vsainternational.org*

First Published 2025 by Indie Experts Publishing

Published by Indie Experts Publishing & Author Services

Curated by Dixie Maria Carlton
www.indieexpertspublishing.com

Cover design and typesetting by
Ammie Christiansen, Fast Forward Design
www.fastforwarddesign.co.nz

Typeset in 11pt Minion Pro

ISBN:

978-1-7386102-0-4 (Printed)
978-1-7386102-3-5 (eBook)

Dedication:

For everyone who's ever sat in a conference clutching a notebook, scribbling furiously, only to later wonder, "What on earth did I mean by that squiggly arrow?"

This book is for you—the note-takers, the highlighters, the "I'll definitely remember this bit" optimists—who wished you could bottle the brilliance of the day and take it home intact.

Here, at last, is the conference you won't forget—your Conference in a Book™.

CONTENTS

Welcome

BY DIXIE MARIA CARLTON

Have you ever attended a truly transformative business conference? The kind where you leave not just with notes but with new perspectives, renewed energy, and a stack of ideas ready to implement?

Now imagine capturing that experience—all the insight, inspiration, and impact—from the comfort of your own space, at your own pace.

That's exactly what this book delivers.

Connect, Lead, Succeed is not just a book. It's a curated, global event in written form. A "Conference in a Book." Within these pages, you'll meet world-class thought leaders, keynote speakers, and transformational coaches from around the world—each bringing their best ideas to the stage, one chapter at a time.

Each section opens with the same spirit as if you were sitting in the front row, listening to a brilliant speaker walk onto stage, ready to deliver their keynote. As you turn the page, it's as if you're hearing them speak directly to you—on leadership, teams, culture, technology, mindset, communication, and the future of business.

This book was created to serve not just as a collection of ideas but as a powerful platform for those who live to share their expertise and guide others through change. Whether you're a CEO, entrepreneur, educator, or conference organizer looking for the next generation of keynote speakers, these are the people you'll want to know.

So, take your time. Dog-ear the pages. Highlight the insights. Share the quotes. Refer back as often as you need.

And if you're in the business of events and transformation, let this be your backstage pass to some of the best minds in the speaking world—right here, ready to help you and your teams connect more deeply, lead more authentically, and succeed more meaningfully.

Welcome to the conference. You're already in the front row.

— *Dixie Carlton*
Founder, Indie Experts Publishing
Global Speaker Coach & Strategist
Creator of the "Conference in a Book"™ Series

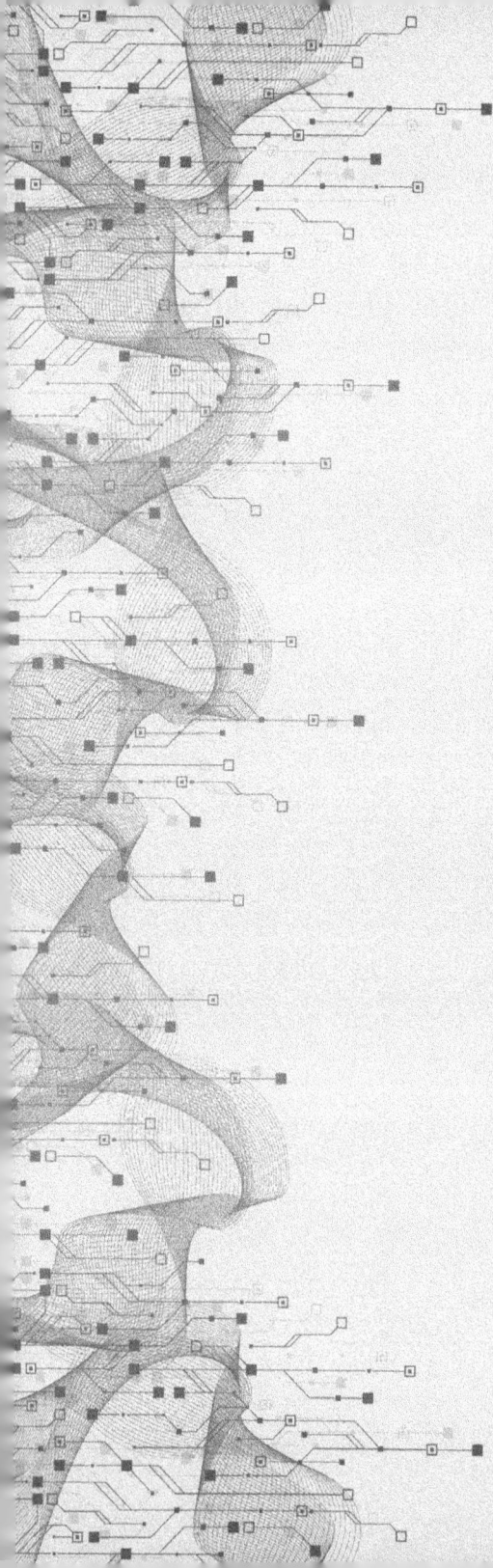

SESSION ONE

Leadership

Limor Jasinski

Antoni Lacinai

Dr Stephen Morse

Marta Pardo

Dr Wendy Lee

Welcome to the Leadership Session

Ladies and gentlemen, welcome to the first session of our "Conference in a Book" experience. This is where we begin—with leadership. And not just leadership in the traditional sense. Here, we explore what it means to lead with heart, with clarity, and with a deep understanding of the human experience behind every business, project, or purpose-driven mission.

In this powerful opening lineup, we've brought together some of the most inspiring voices from around the world, each offering a unique lens on leadership for a rapidly changing world.

*We begin with **Limor Jasinski**, a mindset coach and founder of Wisdom Kids Academy, who reminds us that leadership doesn't start in the boardroom—it starts in childhood. Her keynote, Redefining Leadership, explores the idea that our next generation of CEOs, changemakers, and team leaders are being shaped today in classrooms, homes, and everyday moments of emotional courage. She brings stories and strategies that show how building leadership from the inside out starts far earlier than most of us realize.*

*Next up, we shift gears with **Antoni Lacinai**, a Swedish communication expert and international speaker, whose keynote From Hands to Head to Heart takes us on a journey through the evolution of leadership—moving away from micromanagement and command-and-control, toward trust, engagement, and human-centered performance. With humor, insight, and practical tools, Antoni lays out how soft skills deliver hard results.*

Then we welcome **Dr. Stephen Morse**, *founder of Unchained Solutions, who takes us into the heart of impact leadership. In From Risk to Responsibility, he challenges us to lead beyond compliance and toward conscious capitalism—addressing modern slavery, ESG strategies, and how small businesses can step up in big ways. His message? Sustainable leadership is no longer optional.*

We meet **Marta Pardo**, *known as The Audacious Vroomer, whose decades of international leadership and motorsport grit are distilled into the high-energy P-ROAD Method. She explores how motivation, self-awareness, and team performance are supercharged when leaders learn to read their people like engines—and fuel them accordingly.*

And finally, we hear from **Dr. Wendy Lee**, *She's a Certified Speaking Professional, the founder of Chapter One Asia, and the visionary behind the world's first BrandImage™ Institute. Get ready to experience her signature blend of science, substance, and style — because when Dr. Wendy takes the stage, presence isn't just taught, it's felt.*

So, buckle in. This is the Leadership Session. These are your keynote speakers. And this is your invitation to lead not just with influence, but with intention.

Let's get started.

Introducing Limor Jasinski, Poland

Our first speaker is a pioneer in redefining what leadership *really* means—and when it truly begins. Limor Jasinski is a certified youth mindset coach, founder of Wisdom Kids Academy, and Warsaw's leading expert in building confidence, emotional resilience, and self-leadership in children and teens. With over a decade of coaching experience, she's here to remind us that the leaders of tomorrow are shaped by the conversations we're having today—at home, in schools, and in those small, defining moments of childhood.

Please welcome the inspiring Limor Jasinski!

CHAPTER ONE

Redefining Leadership

*What if the whole future of
leadership depends on what we
teach our children today?*

Starting at the Beginning

We spend billions training adults to become better leaders.

Executive retreats. Coaching programs. Conferences. Book after book after book.

And for good reason.

Leadership affects everything: culture, performance, morale, innovation.

But what if we've misunderstood when leadership actually begins?

It's something I've been wondering about for years now. We say leadership is a skill, so why do we wait so long to teach it?

A recent study by Brandon Hall Group, a respected research and advisory firm, found that **seven out of ten organizations believe leadership training is** *essential for every employee,* **not just for top executives.** This means businesses are finally waking up to a truth long overlooked: that leadership is not a luxury but a necessity.

That study stuck with me. But it also raised a bigger, bolder question in my mind: if leadership is so vital that businesses pour resources into developing it across all levels of their organization, why are we waiting until adulthood to start teaching it?

- **Why are we waiting** until workplace conflict, burnout, or performance pressure pushes us to develop emotional intelligence and self-awareness?

- **Why aren't we cultivating** those qualities *much earlier,* when our brains are still growing, our belief systems are still forming, and our identity is still being shaped?

For far too long, we've misunderstood leadership. We've treated it like a milestone you strive to reach only after degrees, experience, and applause.

But what if leadership isn't something we arrive at... but something we learn to grow into? I think it's time to redefine leadership.

I believe it begins somewhere else entirely...

Not in corner offices or company strategy sessions, but in the in-between moments of childhood. At the dinner table. On the playground. In messy mistakes and quiet choices.

A child navigating a friendship fallout. Standing up to a classmate. Soothing a younger sibling. These aren't just behavioral moments—they are early signals of something deeper: the emerging capacity to lead oneself, for better or worse. And when children are taught essential mindset skills, they begin to develop emotional awareness and leadership from the inside out.

I recently witnessed a touching moment when a 10-year-old comforted a classmate who got his finger stuck in the door. He sat beside him, embraced him, and encouraged him to take deep breaths. Slowly, the boy calmed down. This simple act of compassion was a beautiful example of unrefined yet genuine leadership.

The truth is **kids are already leading.** They're managing emotions, navigating relationships, solving problems, speaking up—or choosing silence—with consequences. They are constantly practicing leadership. We just don't always recognize it for what it is.

And that raises some questions:

- What would change if we did recognize it?
- What if we began to see everyday acts of courage, empathy, and self-regulation not as *growing up*, but as the early architecture of leadership?
- What if leadership development didn't begin with seminars but with **self-trust**, taught in childhood?

Because when we see leadership as an early skill to teach and nurture, we don't just help kids behave better. We raise better leaders who are grounded, self-aware, emotionally intelligent, *and resilient.*

And right now, the world needs those kinds of leaders more than ever.

According to the **World Health Organization**, one in seven adolescents globally experiences a mental health disorder. In the US, **emergency room visits for suspected suicide attempts among teens rose by 31%** in 2020. And those numbers keep climbing.

More than **70% of teens** report feeling overwhelmed by anxiety, peer pressure, and fear of failure, often triggered by a constant stream of social comparison and disconnection.

These are warning signals not only for the mental health crisis affecting our children, but also for the kind of leaders we are (or aren't) raising.

Many of us grew up without the tools to manage our own thoughts, emotions, and internal world. We weren't taught what to do with fear, failure, or big emotions. We learned to suppress, avoid, or perfect. *Our parents, and their parents before them, were shaped by wars, economic hardship, and cultural taboos around vulnerability.* Emotional intelligence wasn't a priority; it was a luxury. But that avoidance has trickled down, and now our children are bearing the cost.

And now?

We find ourselves trying to *re-learn* leadership as adults, when so much of our inner narrative is already baked in.

But here's the good news. Empathy, emotional intelligence, compassion, and tolerance—these are skills. And skills can be taught.

Dr Carol Dweck's landmark research on **growth mindset** shows that when children believe their abilities can develop through effort and strategy, they become more resilient, curious, and confident. They take more risks, recover faster from setbacks, and *lead themselves*, even in difficulty.

The **CASEL framework**, one of the most respected models for social and emotional learning, confirms that when children learn core mindset and emotional regulation skills early, they experience:

- better academic performance
- healthier relationships
- lower stress and anxiety
- and a stronger sense of self-worth.

These are foundational leadership competencies.

Which brings us to a critical turning point in this conversation…

If the future of leadership depends on our ability to grow confident, emotionally resilient, and self-aware leaders, why aren't we starting when it counts most?

In early childhood, in middle school, in those messy, beautiful years when beliefs are formed, values are absorbed, and identity is shaped.

This is where **my work** lives.

As a certified kids and teen mindset coach, I've spent years guiding children through the inner process of building confidence, courage, emotional strength, and a sense of identity rooted in self-trust.

Through that work, I've seen leadership as a kind of **inner architecture**, something we build from the foundation up.

It begins not with rules and rewards but with **connection, validation, accountability, belief rewiring**, and, eventually, **empowered self-leadership**. These aren't just leadership skills; they're emotional blueprints children carry into adult life.

That's what my BRAVE framework is all about, and we'll explore it through real stories and lived coaching experiences later in this chapter.

But before we dive into the "how," let's go deeper into the "who." If leadership truly begins in childhood, what role do we, as adults, play in shaping it?

The Role of Adults

The other night, during dinner, I was toggling between parenting and trying to steal a quiet moment on Netflix. I must've paused a dozen times—helping my son with a loose tooth, slicing vegetables, answering questions. Then came one more "Mom?"—and I snapped. Sharp tone. Short fuse. "*What?*"

I saw it instantly. His eyes dropped. His shoulders slumped. His spark disappeared.

I apologized, then blamed the mouse on the screen. "It's not you," I told him. But deep down, we both knew it was. I didn't want to hurt his feelings, so I deflected. I thought I was protecting him by softening the truth a little.

Later that night, as I lay in bed replaying that moment, I realized something painful yet powerful: the real harm hadn't come from snapping. It had come from "softening the truth." I had blamed the mouse instead of owning my reaction. But what I actually did was far more damaging. I taught my son to second-guess his emotional reality.

He knew I snapped at him because he interrupted me during a moment of tiredness at the end of a long day. But when I denied it, I made him doubt what he felt. I didn't just avoid responsibility. I confused his inner compass. And without that compass, how can a child learn to trust themselves? How can they develop the confidence to make good decisions?

That was the moment I understood something I'll never forget.

Our children don't need us to be perfect. They need us to be honest with our feelings and theirs, especially when it's uncomfortable.

Kindness without honesty isn't protection. It's distortion.

Our children don't need us to be perfect. They need us to be honest with our feelings and theirs, especially when it's uncomfortable.

The next day, we talked. I told him he was right to feel as he did the previous night. I explained what had happened and why it mattered. That moment didn't make me a perfect parent. Just a conscious one. And I believe *that's* what changes everything. It's the willingness to reflect, to repair, and to take responsibility that turns everyday mistakes into moments of growth.

Children don't develop emotional strength by accident. They learn it by watching us.

- They watch how we manage frustration.
- They see how we repair after a mistake.
- They hear how we speak to ourselves when we mess up.
- They notice when we avoid.
- And they absorb when we take responsibility.

Developmental psychologists like **Morris Massey** have long emphasized the "**Modelling Period**" of childhood (ages 8–13), a phase where children are especially shaped by the adults they admire most. **In those years, our everyday choices become their blueprint for what leadership looks like.**

Children don't develop emotional strength by accident. They learn it by watching us.

So, yes, many of us weren't raised with these tools. We're still learning them in real time. We're healing wounds from our childhoods, trying to respond differently from the ways we inherited. And that's not weakness. That's **generational strength** in action.

Because doing the personal work—learning to regulate ourselves, speak the truth in love, and model emotional courage—doesn't just make us better parents. It redefines what leadership looks like for the next generation.

It goes far beyond parenting. **Every adult in a child's life is a leader.** Whether you're a teacher, mentor, coach, older sibling, aunt, uncle, or manager—if a child looks up to you, your influence matters.

We all influence children.
The only real question is whether we're doing it with
intention—or by default.

So, what can we do—especially when we don't have all the answers?

One powerful way adults can lead by example is by seeking support, especially when we know we lack the tools or language to teach these skills on our own. And that's where a new and growing profession is making a difference: youth life coaching. Most of us are familiar with life coaching for adults, whether in business, sports, or personal development. But **life coaching for children and teens** is still relatively new. And it's quickly becoming one of the most impactful ways to support emotional development and confidence.

In my coaching practice, I work with kids and teens to help them understand how their mind works, how to manage their emotions, and how they can build the kind of self-leadership that will shape every area of their lives.

Just as a parent might hire a math tutor or a tennis coach, they can also turn to a certified kids coach to help their child develop the skills, confidence, and ability to thrive in life. Remember, seeking help is not a sign of weakness but a sign of strength and a commitment to growth.

When we lead that way—with courage, humility, and heart—we're not just raising children.

We're raising future leaders.

Coaching Future Leaders—
One Story at a Time

If what we teach our children today determines the kind of leaders they'll become tomorrow, then how do we raise a generation with a strong sense of self *before* the louder voices of the world drown out their inner wisdom?

When I think about what leadership looks like in real life, I often see it through the eyes of the children I coach.

Every child I work with comes to me carrying something different. For some, it's lack of confidence. For others, it's the fear of failing or making a mistake. Some feel pressure to fit in, or they struggle to say no. And for others, it's the heavy shadow of anxiety.

But at the heart of it all, I often find the same fragile truth: ***they haven't yet discovered the power they hold within.***

Most children don't *question* their thoughts or feelings—they *believe* them. They believe that fear means danger, a mistake means failure, and a thought means truth. They've never been taught that their inner world can be understood, shaped, or even changed. They don't yet know that courage can be practiced, confidence can be developed, and calm can be created from within.

Leah was one of those children. When I first received her intake form, I paused. At just 11 years old, she had already lived in multiple countries, navigating different cultures, languages, and environments. While that brought her richness, it also exposed her to uncertainty, change—and distressing global events. Her parents described high levels of anxiety, daily panic episodes, and a growing sense of helplessness. I questioned whether I was the right person to help and whether coaching alone would be enough. But her parents weren't looking for more therapy; they were looking for hope, for different tools, and for a new kind of support.

What followed became one of the most profound coaching journeys I've ever witnessed. It was during this time that my *Inner Architecture of Leadership* framework came into full expression, captured in the acronym **BRAVE**, which distills five core pillars into a clear, coachable model for transformation.

Developed over years of guiding children through their most vulnerable moments, BRAVE came to life in my sessions with Leah—alongside the proven tools of the *Adventures in Wisdom*™ story-based curriculum, a powerful system that teaches 27 mindset skills through stories, conversations, and fun hands-on activities. As I helped Leah understand how her mind works, how to manage her fears, and how to build emotional resilience, the deeper journey of BRAVE unfolded organically.

Let me walk you through Leah's transformation using **BRAVE**:

B - Begin with Trust:

The first step was to create a safe space for Leah, a judgement-free environment where trust could be built. This safe space was the foundation for understanding and managing her anxiety. In a collaborative process, we created a roadmap for her success.

I helped Leah familiarize herself with her emotions by explaining how her brain works, how thoughts create feelings, and how fear is not a flaw but an alert signal. In ways she could understand and connect with, I introduced simple models about the mind, including belief systems and how our subconscious mind works.

R - Recognize and Validate Emotions:

One of the most powerful shifts came through validation. Leah didn't need someone to tell her everything was "okay." She needed someone to say, *"What you feel is real. And you're not crazy for feeling it."* We talked about the kinds of fears many kids experience—like worrying about their parents dying or some other terrible thing happening—and I assured her that these thoughts, while scary, are more common than most people admit. We gently explored them. No judgment. Just truth, spoken with care. And in that space, her walls began to come down.

A - Accountability and Ownership:

Leah began to realize that her thoughts, while powerful, weren't in charge. She was. One of our most impactful tools was the creation of her "Fear Box." Whenever a fearful or anxious thought surfaced, she'd write it down, place it in the box, and let it go. Later, she asked if we could burn the notes. "It'll feel like they're gone forever," she said. That was her moment of ownership. Not denial or victimhood but *actions*. She took charge of the stories she used to believe and began creating new ones. These are the seeds of leadership.

V - Value-Centered Repair:

A big part of our work was helping Leah repair her relationship with herself. Her fears and anxiety had created disconnection from her body, her confidence, and her sense of inner peace. I taught her a tapping technique and guided visualizations to bring her back to the present moment. She began to say to herself things like "I'm here. I'm safe. I'm loved." These practices helped her feel calm, brave, and capable and to reconnect with her inner knowing and with the people around her. And when she saw it—really saw and felt it—her confidence grew. She no longer viewed herself as someone with anxiety. She viewed herself as someone who could handle it.

E - Empowered Self-Leadership:

Over time, Leah didn't just learn to manage her anxiety; she began to lead herself through it. She would recognize the early signs, apply the tools, and stay grounded. She started encouraging her friends, even sharing some of the calming tools she had learned with her sister. That's when I knew this wasn't just confidence but leadership in action.

This is what **BRAVE** looks like in real life. This is what mindset coaching makes possible.

It's not about fixing kids or replacing the role of the parent. It's about creating a support system with a certified professional coach. It's about giving them tools—language, insight, and a safe environment where they can see themselves as capable, powerful, and whole.

This is the work I do through *Wisdom Kids Academy*, the youth mindset coaching practice I founded in Warsaw. As a certified Wisdom Coach using the Adventures in Wisdom™ curriculum, I offer one-on-one coaching, parent and school workshops, and leadership clubs for kids and teens, teaching the skills most adults never learned.

If you're a parent whose child is struggling, you don't have to figure it out on your own.

If you're an educator or school leader looking for new ways to support your students' well-being, I invite you to bring this work to your classrooms. Book a workshop. Start a club. Let's build future leaders together.

And if you're someone who feels called to make a difference in the lives of children, I invite you to explore this work and perhaps even become a kids' coach yourself.

Leadership is not a privilege saved for the children of tomorrow; it is the vital foundation we nurture in them today.

Limor

About Limor Jasinski

Limor Jasinski is a passionate speaker, youth empowerment coach, and founder of **Wisdom Kids Academy**, dedicated to helping young people unlock their full potential through inner leadership, resilience, and emotional intelligence.

With a warm, relatable presence and a deep understanding of what drives confidence in children and teens, Limor has become a trusted voice for parents, schools, and educators seeking meaningful change in how youth are supported and inspired. Drawing from her own journey and a background in personal development, Limor delivers impactful keynotes and workshops that speak directly to the hearts of young people—igniting self-belief, purpose, and the courage to dream big.

Limor works internationally with schools, youth programs, and community leaders, delivering age-appropriate talks for students aged 10–18, as well as sessions for teachers, parents, and corporate graduate programs. Her work is grounded in her belief that when young people connect with their inner wisdom and emotional strength, they don't just succeed—they lead.

Whether she's on stage in front of hundreds or guiding a workshop of curious minds, Limor brings clarity, energy, and compassion to every audience she serves. She is on a mission to raise a generation of wise, resilient, and heart-led leaders—one school, one child, and one powerful conversation at a time.

www.wisdom-kidsacademy.com

Introducing Antoni Lacinai, Sweden

Up next is a speaker who brings heart, science, and strategy into every conversation. Antoni Lacinai is an international keynote speaker, communication expert, and author based in Sweden. With a background in leadership and behavioral science, he helps teams thrive through empathy, clarity, and energy—his signature formula for high-impact communication. Whether you're leading meetings or movements, Antoni's insights will help you turn strategy into action and good intentions into great culture. With 25+ years of experience on global stages and his upcoming book CARE, he's here to remind us: when you lead with kindness, people lean in—and results follow.

CHAPTER TWO

From Hands to Head to Heart

The Future of
Human-Centered Leadership

ere is a question for you: Are your team doing their daily tasks because they *want to*, or because they *have to*? Or, as one of my previous clients said after they hired to me speak to their top 200 executives, "*We have already had some of that employee engagement fluff before. But now it's about getting shit done!*" He was somewhat taken aback when I explained that, actually, you get shit done better and faster if people are engaged. That it is about moving toward your strategies and goals by exercising a servant mindset, a positive attitude, and great communication skills—or, in short, soft skills for hard results.

We are at a crossroads right now, where some leaders will choose command-and-control, distrusting their people and treating them like machines or spare parts. We've spent decades managing people as if they were. Add some whips and carrots (often minus the carrots), and you get a micromanaging leader and an exhausting workplace. And what do you get in return? Exactly what you ask for. People clock in, do their task, and clock out. No creativity, no initiatives, no accountability. So you add more whips, more threats, more intimidation. The team will probably perform better because it works—for a while. But it is not sustainable.

This chapter is for you who understand that if you want sustainable growth, you need to get people engaged and motivated, so that they perform willingly. **It's about moving away from clenched fists and toward helping hands.** I want you to be a world-class leader, where you meet, greet, and treat people with care and enthusiasm. I want you to serve your team, so that they serve your mission, especially if you care for them, for your clients, and for the planet. I want you to lead with your heart, cultivating a workplace of collaboration and connection and showing trust in your teams. And trust is the currency of leadership.

Let's go on a quick historical tour:

Managing hands - The outdated era of leadership

If you look at human history from a couple of hundred thousand years ago up until very recently, the ideal worker was obedient, efficient, and replaceable. Just like spare parts. One breaks down? Find another. Injuries? Replace. Protests? Fire and hire new. You want more output? Add more hands. And to no one's surprise you get a disengaged workforce doing only what they have to. They stop thinking. They stop caring for anything more than getting paid. And it is very seldom their fault. This command-and-control style that we still see in a lot of places around the world is all about leading hands with hands (or fists).

One of the worst examples of management by terror that I have ever heard happened in 2008. A CEO of a large company with about

150,000 employees decided to get rid of more than 20,000 of them to increase profit for the shareholders. Now, this was in France, and you cannot fire people easily. But this clever man thought long and hard until he came up with the perfect solution. He gathered his executive team and said (I am paraphrasing him) *"We will bully them out of the company! Relocate them. Give them useless tasks. Move them to locations they don't want to live in. Make them feel worthless. Then they will quit by themselves. Mark my words: they will leave, either through the door or through the window!"*

Eleven years later, the CEO was fined and sent to prison (for only a few months). Why? More than 19 people were so broken down mentally that they chose the window...

From Hands to Heads: When brains matter more than muscles

As we then moved into the knowledge economy, people went from manufacturing to marketing, and from production to Power-Points. Leadership changed. Many went from tasks and commands (hands) to strategies and plans (heads). This is a good next step in the evolution. When you lead with your head, you are able to use the collective intelligence of your team. There is often more room for innovation in things like how to better serve clients. But with the knowledge economy comes the suffering of ineffective meetings, (many) filled with a massive number of deadly boring slides and incomprehensible Excel spreadsheets. It is a limbo state between hands and hearts, so I will not dwell here for much longer. It's like music on CDs, filling a gap between LPs and streaming services. Let's just agree that slides and plans and strategies very seldom *move* you or get you passionate about peak performing. There is no spark in documents with abstract language or forgotten relics called "Our Values" on a roll-up, or in the cloud, with no real meaning. And we crave meaning. We can see signs of Quiet Quitting, meaning that people make only minimum effort, or Quiet Resignation, where people just leave their jobs. And now there's Coffee Badging, where people show up at the office just for show, do nothing meaningful, and then leave.

One old example of this is the legendary story from the harbor in Gothenburg where one man spent his days carrying a plank over his shoulder. Nobody ever saw him do any work, ever.

From Heads to Hearts: Inspire engagement, lead with CARE

If the illusion of control hadn't already been exposed, 2020 is when it collapsed. We weren't in the same room anymore so we couldn't physically watch people work. We had to trust them. We had to listen more and direct less. Leadership had to grow up. That's where the "heart" comes in. Sure, there are some backlashes, hence the crossroads I mentioned in the beginning. As I am writing this, we see a shift back to leading with clenched fists instead of helping hands. This will not end well. Promoting people based on their abilities to *commute* more than their ability to contribute is dumb, and it is super easy to pretend to work in a physical location too.

The ABCs of psychological needs

Leading with your heart is about leading with CARE (I'll come back to the CARE concept at the end). It is also about understanding the ABCs of psychological needs that people have (based on Self-Determination Theory, a branch within psychology).

The theory hinges on three key concepts:

- **Autonomy** – This is the sweet spot where coaching and delegating resides. People don't want you to micromanage them, but they don't want you to abdicate either. If you stop caring, they soon will too.

- **Belonging** – This is perhaps the strongest driving force of humanity. We crave being part of a tribe, a village, a community where we feel appreciated and a part of something bigger than ourselves. If you can create a WE-culture instead of a ME-culture, you will increase collaboration and output tenfold.

- **Competence** – Most of us want to grow and show our

competence, spiritually, mentally, and physically. We want to develop and learn. We want to feel significant.

I have coached thousands of leaders and teams, and, based on my experience, the best leaders always promote autonomy, belonging, and competence. Head-based leadership isn't enough. Strategy without empathy is cold. Vision without connection doesn't land. The real transformation comes when we also lead with the **heart**—with trust, empathy, and real human connection. When we care, engagement lives. When we care, people grow. And this is where performance becomes sustainable.

Let's look at four pillars of heart-based leadership.

1: Instill psychological safety by having a green light mindset

Imagine a traffic light in your brain. Depending on which light is dominant, you will have different thoughts, feelings, and communication with people. Let's go through them briefly.

- **Red light** – This is what psychologist Paul Gilbert calls the Threat System. If this goes bananas, we want to escape from a dangerous environment, so we will either attack or run away. Massive volumes of cortisol are pumped out, and we cannot think clearly. This is where toxic cultures and workplaces exist with management leading by terror and intimidation (leading with clenched fists).

- **Yellow light** – This is where we find the drive to explore. We search for opportunities, and we seek ways to reach our goals. When we succeed, we are rewarded with dopamine and feel good for a short while, until we start hunting for more. Too much of this might lead to burnout and high frustration, especially when roles, goals, and mandates are unclear (management by reorganization), so be careful of leading teams with this as the only motivator.

- **Green light** – Here you are at ease. You are not threatened, you enjoy your job, and life is just good and restful. There is a high flow of oxytocin all over. Be careful, though. Too much of this and the team will lose energy and courage. You might end up in a managing-by-not-rocking-the-boat scenario. It could quickly lead to stagnation.

A green light mindset and culture creates psychological safety, and it is the **#1 predictor** of high-performing teams. Why? Because when people feel safe, they speak up. They solve problems. They admit errors and fix them. Creativity goes up. Accidents go down. Innovation increases. Absenteeism decreases. Without safety, workers follow rules and commands instead of sharing ideas. And that's dangerous. You don't need to be perfect to build safety. You just need to be **available** and **kind**—asking questions and listening to understand, not to respond.

2: Build trust by focusing on empathy

Trust is the oxygen of leadership. It doesn't mean agreement. It means believing that people have your back—and that you have theirs. That requires empathy and emotional intelligence: the ability to notice what's going on beneath the surface and respond with care, not control.

Studies have shown that if you have executives with perceived high levels of empathy, you get around 70% of the workforce being engaged or highly engaged, compared with only 15%–30% if they are not. And engagement is the key that unlocks performance and great results.

Utilizing soft skills is not about being soft. Because business runs on relationships. Soft skills, therefore, equal hard results.

3: Increase engagement with praise, purpose, and fun

Job satisfaction means you don't hate your job. Engagement means you **love** contributing. It's active. It's emotional. It's energetic. Engaged employees use their initiative. They bring ideas. They care about the higher purpose and outcomes. Gallup's global data shows that highly engaged teams are 21% more profitable and 59% less likely to leave. Some reports also show that less than one quarter of the workforce are what they call actively engaged, meaning that people go above and beyond. Let's agree that there is potential for improvement here.

How do you spark engagement? Praise people when they do well. According to an IBM study, high performing teams attract six times more positive recognition than the average teams, while low-performing teams attract twice the negative recognition.

Ping-pong tables (as a metaphor) is another way. It's fun, and fun at work has all sorts of positive effects. You can also increase engagement with communicating a clear purpose and by involving people more than you inform them. People want to feel valued. I also want to add that the real problem is not the people who are "merely satisfied." They might enjoy their boss, their colleagues, and their work, but still, it's a job and they have other interests too. Your real worry are the saboteurs, the ones who create hate, fear, and polarization. They make the team as a whole about 30% less productive, and people around a saboteur will suffer greatly.

4: Leverage the three communication superpowers

In my keynotes, masterclasses, and coaching programs, I always speak about the three communication superpowers. If you master them, you have a shot at being nothing less than a world-class leader. Fun fact: you will also come across as more charismatic, thus increasing your influence and impact!

The superpowers are:

- **Energy** – so that people believe that you believe (why should they believe if you don't?), and this is mostly visible in your non-verbal communication; i.e., how you look and how you sound when you communicate. Energy is like a magnet. If you have it, people gravitate towards you.

- **Empathy** – so that people connect with you and feel that you get them, that you are present, and that you are interested instead of interesting. It is here that real trust and loyalty is created. It is here you win people—and business.
- **Clarity** – so that they get you and remember what you said. It's about being simple but still having substance. This is not easy. Most people complicate the shit out of things with abbreviations and buzz words, which just makes people feel stupid. Make them feel smart and they will follow you anywhere.

My advice: start with empathy so that you know who you are talking to. Then craft a compelling message with clarity. Finally, deliver it with the right energy to boost inspiration. And don't think that one of the superpowers is enough. Clarity without empathy makes you a dominant asshole. Energy without clarity makes you a clown. Empathy without energy makes you a therapist. It is only together that they create magic.

Here is an example of what can happen when you use empathy in your business. I was giving a one-day masterclass in the three communication superpowers to a real estate company who had issues with their tenants. There were lots of complaints and an overall bad atmosphere. We put a lot of focus on empathy. I got an email from the client after a few weeks. It went something like this: *"It's amazing. Our tenants seem to like us now! All we did was to listen more. And the cool thing is: Now we like them too!"*

Knowing how to meet, greet, and treat your colleagues in a positive way will impact your bottom line. As I said: soft skills get hard results.

Leadership That Lasts

Leadership isn't about keeping a machine running. It's about growing people. Helping them become more than they were yesterday. Creating spaces where clarity, connection, and care are the norm. You don't need to be perfect. Just present. Curious. Clear. Using a green light mindset and communication. Being willing to lead from both the head and the heart.

This is how you build trust.

This is how you shape culture.

This is how you leave people better than you found them.

And it doesn't stop with your team. It extends forward—to the teams they'll lead, the people they'll mentor, the families they'll go home to. Your leadership will affect not only your own team, but also people you haven't even met. It's called emotional contagion. You are like a rock that plummets into the ocean. The wave is your influence and the emotions you stir up. So why not be a superspreader of joy, care, and connection? Why not be a large rock instead of a grain of sand? Foster new leaders in a CARE-centric culture and you will have a legacy. This is generativity in action.

When we lead well today, we invest in generations ahead. Let's be the kind of leaders they'll thank—even if they never know your name.

Want to go deeper?

As I am writing this for you, I am also co-writing a whole book together with Daniela Landherr, an awesome human being and leadership development expert. Our working title is *CARE*, and it is a strategic leadership book about what you gain when you lead with care and with the heart. It is about building trust, engagement, and impact through the right attitude and great communication. In it, you'll discover a new blueprint called the CARE concept and how to utilize:

- **Connect** – so that you create a real relationship, not just transactions
- **Amplify** – so that you celebrate progress, effort, and growth

- **Reflect** – so that you dare to take a step back and together find your way forward
- **Energize** – to light the spark that keeps people moving with meaning

Thank you for reading my mind. Keep leading with your heart. The world will be a better place when you do.

Antoni

Special Bonus
Scan the QR code to access your exclusive bonus material

About Antoni Lacinai

Antoni Lacinai is an international keynote speaker, author, and communication expert based in Sweden. With a background in leadership and behavioral science, he helps leaders and teams communicate with more empathy, clarity, and energy—three words that have become the foundation of his work. Or as his tagline goes: Communication made easy, so that your strategies become reality.

His clients are often ambitious, caring leaders in HR or other executive roles who want to improve collaboration, trust, and engagement in their teams. Through keynotes, masterclasses, and hands-on training, he shows how better conversations can lead to better results.

Antoni is often interviewed in the media and contributes regularly as a columnist, sharing insights on conscious leadership, motivation, and workplace culture. Audiences appreciate his ability to make complex ideas simple, relatable, and actionable.

With over 25 years of experience on stages around the world, he has developed tools and stories that move people—from knowing to doing, and from doing to caring. His upcoming book *CARE* introduces a new model for modern leadership: Connect, Attract, Recognize, Energize.

Whether in a boardroom or on a big stage, his message is clear: *You have nothing to lose by being kind.*

Get more inspiration on ***www.antonilacinai.com*** and linkedin.com/in/Lacinai and get templates, books, and checklists here to elevate yourself even more: antonilacinai.com/downloadable-material.

Introducing Dr. Stephen Morse, Australia

Our next speaker is a leader who proves that ethics and enterprise are not opposites—they're partners. Dr. Stephen Morse is the CEO of Unchained Solutions, a Sydney-based B-Corp helping businesses align ESG strategy with real-world impact. With a doctorate in Human Trafficking Intervention and decades of experience in leadership across sectors, Stephen works with companies to go beyond compliance and tackle modern slavery and sustainability at their core. He's here to challenge us: What does it really mean to lead with purpose in a global economy? Get ready for a conversation that's bold, inspiring, and grounded in real responsibility.

CHAPTER THREE

From Risk Management to Meaningful Impact

The New Paradigm of
Sustainable Leadership

Hidden Risks, Visible Impact

In May 2022, the oil tanker AG Neptune was detained off the coast of Newcastle, Australia. It was carrying 62,000 tons of diesel fuel from Taiwan—fuel, it turned out, that had been contaminated with seawater, causing an estimated AU$75 million loss. But this financial disaster concealed a much more troubling reality. Authorities discovered 21 seafarers on board working in shocking conditions that breached the Maritime Labour Convention: unpaid wages exceeding AU$120,000, inadequate food and water, poor medical care, and overall substandard living conditions [1]

The *AG Neptune* was banned from Australian waters for six months—a rare and serious sanction. But for one of our clients, the real impact wasn't just the contaminated diesel or the legal penalties. It was the sudden and sobering realization that their supply chain—trusted until then—was implicated in a human rights crisis. This case underscored a fundamental truth: the risks businesses face today extend well beyond balance sheets and operational performance. They are deeply human, profoundly environmental, and often hidden in plain sight.

Such incidents highlight the hidden nature of forced labor, a global issue that often goes unnoticed. In Australia, we have a growing list of reporting frameworks around environmental and human rights due diligence. Their purpose is to help companies make a positive impact on both people and the planet. One key piece of legislation is the Modern Slavery Act 2018(Cth), which calls upon companies to take responsibility for the origins of the goods they source and ensure fair treatment of rights holders throughout their supply base. The Act is part of a rapidly emerging regulatory landscape, the strongest being the EU Corporate Sustainability Reporting Due Diligence Directive, which came into effect in 2024.

Working with Corporates

Since 2019, more than 22,000 Australian organizations (as of April 2025), both large and small, have been reporting to the Attorney-General's Department on their efforts to assess and address the risk of modern slavery within their operations and supply chains. Modern slavery, which is essentially "the commodification of people for the purpose of exploitation and financial gain,"[2] often involves the removal of a person's freedom to move, choose, or speak out.

---

1   (cf. Trade Winds, 2022)
2   (cf. Unseen UK)

According to ILO data from 2021, more than 50 million people are trapped in cycles of forced labor and other violations, a sharp increase from 40 million just a decade ago.[3]

Over the past few years, I've observed a range of responses to the requirement to comply with the Act, from significant progress by high-profile companies to a disturbing lack of action by many others. Some companies remain in denial about the issues, while not-for-profits with limited budgets are taking meaningful steps to improve their practices and work with key suppliers to mitigate the risks—all in addition to fulfilling their core social mission.

It's not unusual for me to work with companies that wish this regulation would simply go away. But what gets me out of bed each day is my hope that justice will prevail for the many children, women, and men who are trapped in cycles of exploitation, where the levers for change seem to be stuck in a gooey mess.

From Madrid to the Mission

People often ask how I came to work in the anti-slavery and sustainability space. The answer begins not in boardrooms or legislative chambers, but on the streets of Madrid. In the early 2010s, I was living in Spain, completing my doctoral research into human trafficking, while my wife, Sarah, a health professional, was serving women emerging from forced sex work.

Beneath the ornate façades and party culture lies an underworld of corruption, mafia control, and systemic exploitation.

Madrid, for many, is a postcard city of rich architecture and vibrant culture, famed for being the noisiest city in Europe with traffic jams common even at 1:00 a.m. But beneath the ornate façades and party culture lies an underworld of corruption, mafia control, and

---

3   (cf. ILO 2021)

systemic exploitation. Spain is both a destination and transit hub for trafficked individuals—trafficked into sex work and agriculture, in particular.[4]

It was during this time I met Pablo at a church I started attending. Pablo was an asylum seeker from Congo-Brazzaville, who had arrived in Spain in order to escape persecution. Pablo wasn't enslaved, but he did live under constant surveillance and economic hardship. Though trained as a math teacher, Pablo had little choice but to work from 3:00 a.m. each day, setting up a produce market and earning about three euros an hour. His story echoes countless other stories of migrants whose lives are circumscribed by invisible borders, unjust laws, and indifferent systems. Sadly, when I returned home in 2016, I lost contact with Pablo due to his limited access to technology and my being caught up in rebuilding my life in Australia with my wife and young children.

What continues to puzzle me about my encounter with Pablo, though, is the question of rights and access. For while I was in Spain by choice and enjoying the full rights that (pre-Brexit) came with a British passport, including access to employment, healthcare and voting, Pablo had few choices and few rights as an asylum seeker. His movements were restricted within Madrid's city limits, and he was routinely asked to show his identity documents to the police. Where I got permanent residency immediately upon application, it took Pablo seven years to get temporary residency.

This grassroots exposure to the "supply side" of modern slavery led Sarah and me to ask questions. Who was demanding these services? Who was benefiting from these broken systems?

The answers pointed to systemic failures in governance, business, and culture. And so, on returning to Australia, we founded Unchained Solutions to partner with companies in bridging this gap—transforming risk awareness into proactive leadership.

---

4   (cf. Morse, 2016)

The ESG Shift: From Risk Management to Impact-Driven Leadership

This brings us to consider a crucial shift in the business world: the integration of social and environmental impact into business operations and strategy. In the 21st century, two major shifts have transformed how business leaders integrate social and environmental concerns into their businesses.

The first is well-known: ESG—Environmental, Social, and Governance—which has become a foundational framework for managing and reporting on non-financial risks to improve financial investments. Though the acronym itself is awkward (two adjectives, plus a noun that needs an extra word to make sense: *reporting*, *principles*, *activities*), ESG captures the systems and values behind good governance. It's about managing carbon footprints, ethical sourcing, inclusive hiring, and responsible data use. It began as a compliance lens from the top end of town—often regulatory, sometimes reputational.

There's a profound shift taking place as ESG evolves from a risk management tool into a platform for strategic risk-taking.

But here's the second, more profound, and more recent shift: ESG is evolving from a risk management tool into a platform for strategic risk-taking—a shift from mitigating risk to taking risks that benefit and contribute concretely to people and planet.

This pivot is especially relevant for business leaders today—not just in multinationals, but also in small businesses, particularly those that function as suppliers to other entities. As regulatory frameworks become more complex, and as consumers, partners, and investors demand more than box-ticking, *leaders are being asked not just to avoid harm, but to create positive impact.*

Why this matters for small business leaders

And why does this matter to small business leaders? Well, embedding ESG into your company's DNA isn't just about satisfying compliance checklists to win business. It's about future-proofing your business. A well-integrated ESG strategy makes your operations more agile, more resilient, and more aligned with the long-term interests of stakeholders—employees, clients, investors, and the community.

For small business owners, this shift requires a new type of leadership. Not the kind that simply avoids risk, but the kind that understands which risks are worth taking for the sake of long-term value for people and planet, not just for profit.

Where ESG once meant implementing an anti-bribery policy or running a carbon audit, it now includes questions like:

- What are we doing to contribute to emerging economies?
- How do we create value in underserved communities?
- How do we invest in social and environmental impact as a driver of growth?

This is the move from ESG as *defensive governance* to ESG as *impact strategy.*

ESG Is More Than a Framework—It's a Leadership Philosophy

In the present global economy, the term ESG appears to be waning in currency. For many, it's become a buzzword which needs to be replaced by another term; say, "Conscious Capitalism."[5]

Even in 2025, we've witnessed governments pushing back emission targets and making commitments to diversity.

---

5   (cf. Mackey and Sisodia 2013)

> *As regulatory frameworks become more complex, and as consumers, partners, and investors demand more than box-ticking, leaders are being asked not just to avoid harm but to create positive impact.*

Though ESG may be losing its market sheen as a term, the idea behind it is more vital than ever. It's not just a compliance tool. It's a leadership mindset, a way to embed long-term thinking into every layer of business strategy and operational function.

We've seen this in the rise of impact investor firms like Brightlight, who evaluate companies not just on how well they mitigate risk, but also on how boldly they pursue positive outcomes. According to Samuel Richards from Brightlight, "What we're seeing is a new appetite for risk—not recklessness, but responsibility." Leaders are learning that the best way to navigate complexity is to **embrace purpose**, not just **protect reputation**.

This raises an essential question for today's business owners: what kind of leadership does the future demand?

> *Leaders are learning that the best way to navigate complexity is to embrace purpose, not just protect reputation.*

The answer lies in understanding that ESG is no longer about surviving scrutiny. It's about thriving through contribution—to a safer, fairer, and more sustainable world.

What, When, Then

So, let's break this down.

What: ESG is not just a reporting framework. It is a mindset, a philosophy, a leadership compass...

When: When a company integrates impact into its strategy and culture; when ESG is not peripheral but central...

Then: That company becomes agile, resilient, and ready for whatever comes next.

Let's explore three dimensions of this transformation under three headings:

1. Leadership through Risk-Taking
2. Leadership through Culture-Shaping
3. Leadership through Future-Proofing

Leadership through Risk-Taking

The role of risk in leadership

"You are what you risk," writes Michele Wucker.[6] In the context of ESG, this rings especially true.

> *It's not enough to comply; we must create. Not just defend against the downside—but invest in the upside of doing good.*

Historically, business leaders avoided risk to preserve stability. But today, real leadership requires taking the right risks—for the right reasons. Investing in fair wages, ethical sourcing, or renewable energy may not offer immediate ROI, but these actions build reputational capital, stakeholder trust, and long-term value. ESG-aligned leadership demands intentionality and boldness in how we navigate complexity. It's not enough to comply; we must create. Not just defend against the downside—but invest in the upside of doing good.

The Modern Slavery Act 2018 *(Cth)* in Australia, for example, legally compels *large* Australian companies to report on forced labor

---

6   (Wucker, 2021).

and child labor risks. But increasingly, small businesses are being asked by clients, banks, and investors to meet similar expectations—even in the absence of legal mandates. It's not enough to avoid harm; the standard is now to *do good*. For small businesses, this means re-defining risk. Choosing to shift to ethical suppliers, to invest in sustainable packaging, or to integrate governance policies—even when it's inconvenient—is what distinguishes strategic leaders from reactive managers.

> *"Avoiding risk might keep you safe. But taking the right risk is what makes you significant."*
> — *Dr. Stephen Morse*

Creating real-world outcomes

Many companies throughout the world are working hard to create real-world outcomes for people and planet—companies like Tony's Chocolonely, Thankyou, and Who Gives a Crap. These enterprises all started small but have become leading disrupters in saturated markets. As the sixth edition of the *Chocolate Scorecard* shows, Tony's is a disrupter due to its commitment to working throughout the supply chain to ensure farmers are paid a fair wage. Their concept of due diligence is not to rely simply on what their direct supplier or trading company tells them but to take the lead on making sure the cocoa is sourced ethically and sustainably.[7]

Take Merchgirls, a Melbourne-based apparel company that decided to eliminate single-use plastics—not because the law required it, but because the planet did. They believed in creating a sustainable future for their customers and suppliers. They returned non-compliant shipments, re-educated suppliers, and absorbed higher costs. The payoff? Brand credibility and customer loyalty. Merchgirls were well advanced in their sustainability efforts before working with my

---

7   (cf. Chocolate Scorecard, 2025)

company, Unchained Solutions. Although we helped Merchgirls to develop their ethical policy portfolio and integrate their work into their brand story, in reality, the paperwork was a means to an end— to put into words what they were already doing in order to inform and shape the market.

These are not just ethical choices; they're strategic ones. They reflect leadership that understands how trust and transparency translate into long-term value.

"Taking risks for people and planet isn't radical. It's responsible." — Dr. Stephen Morse

---

Risk with a human face

The *AG Neptune* incident reinforced this for me. It was about more than bad fuel; it was about people. For our client, it was a wake-up call to re-evaluate fuel supply contracts. For us, it reinforced the need for rigorous due diligence, not just on price and quality but on people and process. My friend Pablo was another reminder of the hidden pressures of unjust economic systems. Though he was not enslaved, his daily struggles echoed those of millions of exploited workers globally.

Risk isn't abstract. It wears a human face. ESG leadership means recognizing this—and acting accordingly.

Leadership Through Culture-Shaping

ESG as a cultural imperative

Peter Drucker notably said, "Culture eats strategy for breakfast." I would add, "Culture eats compliance for lunch."

Policies matter. But without a culture of care, they're just paperwork. Leaders must cultivate workplace cultures that value dignity, inclusion, transparency, and accountability. ESG becomes transformational only when it shifts from the spreadsheet to the spirit of an organization.

Australia's endorsement of ILO Convention 190, which upholds every worker's right to a safe and harassment-free workplace, is a legislative benchmark. But translating this into lived experience? That's the job of leadership.

"Policies don't shape culture. People do."
— Paul E. Spector

From tick-box to transformation

In 2024, I learned more about The BUSY Group, a not-for-profit based in Queensland, Australia, as we assisted them with reporting obligations under the UK Modern Slavery Act (2015). In recent years, The BUSY Group has grown from a youth support initiative into a national leader in employment, education, and training services. Its strong, values-driven culture underpins a wide network of programs, from apprenticeship support to alternative education and disability employment. This cultural foundation has enabled The BUSY Group to lead with purpose, especially in areas of social responsibility.

A few years ago, I had the privilege of working with Leprosy Mission Australia. Their team in Melbourne was keen to work closely with their merchandise suppliers based in South Asia. With Unchained Solutions' facilitation, they held virtual workshops to educate micro-suppliers about human rights. They didn't just send out a self-assessment questionnaire and code of conduct to their suppliers—they built bridges. The relational approach transformed fear into partnership.

Tools for sustainability transformation

Culture change doesn't happen overnight. But here are a few tips to get started:

- Present your team with a clear purpose of where you see the company going and how they can take part.
- Gain insights into what your team cares about, their top priorities, current skill level, and appetite to grow.
- Identify the low-hanging fruit that will enable your team to start small and with practical changes (like light bulbs, waste options, etc).
- Embed ESG agenda items in leadership meetings to celebrate staff initiatives and wins and provide training (that each team member can take a lead on).
- Set clear targets (perhaps two or three for the year), create a position statement or two, and once you work out what works, develop some policies and processes to set the standard.

Culture grows at the intersection of communication, consistency, and courage.

Leadership through Future-Proofing

The next generation of leaders

Peter Drucker also said, "The best way to predict the future is to create it."

Tomorrow's leaders must be ESG-literate. They'll need to navigate climate disruptions, AI ethics, cyber risk, and social accountability—not as specialists, but as holistic thinkers.

The Australian government's Climate-Related Financial Disclosure Framework 2025 requires companies to report how climate change affects their financial strategy. While SMEs might not be directly regulated, the pressure is coming—through insurance premiums, procurement requirements, and investor expectations.

Tomorrow's leaders will need to navigate climate disruptions, AI ethics, cyber risk, and social accountability—not as specialists, but as holistic thinkers.

Building impact ecosystems

The Freedom Business Alliance (FBA) is a global network of businesses and organizations dedicated to creating employment opportunities for survivors of human trafficking and those at risk of exploitation. By supporting enterprises that prioritize freedom, dignity, and sustainable livelihoods, FBA aims to leverage the power of business as a force for good in the fight against modern slavery. The alliance offers resources, training, and a collaborative community to help freedom businesses increase their impact across vulnerable communities worldwide.

One proud member of the FBA is House of Diamonds, a social enterprise based in East Java, Indonesia. House of Diamonds was founded by sisters Ida and Lila to sell goods and clothing. As children and teenagers, Ida and Lila faced enormous hardship, but they have demonstrated incredible resilience and self-belief to build a company that enables young, marginalized women in their community to live lives that involve meaningful employment as textile artists in a safe, fun, and loving environment.

Over the past few years, Unchained has formed a partnership with Ida and Lila and other like-minded founders in South-East Asia as part of our long-standing work with the Freedom Business Alliance. Our role has been to provide advice and support to strengthen their approach to policy development and risk management as part of an emerging collective of impacting businesses similar to Social Traders in Australia.

The future belongs to those who build *impact ecosystems,* where clients, suppliers, advisors, and investors are aligned by values, not just through contracts. Certifications like ISO 20400 or B-Corp status are becoming passports to credible leadership.

Culture-driven transformation

The companies that thrive in the future will be those led by culture-shaping, values-driven leaders. ESG shouldn't be the responsibility of a single team; it should be in the DNA of the business.

Risk has been at the center of the journey Sarah and I have taken ever since we explored the issue of human trafficking in Spain in 2010 and morphed into a social enterprise in 2018.

Unchained Solutions exists to unlock the potential of big business in complex industries to neutralize or radically reverse negative impact on the environment and human rights like modern slavery. Since inception, our purpose has been to lead companies beyond compliance and demonstrate our commitment to culture-shaping through the way we create a space for skilled migrants to kickstart their careers, through our engagement with corporate clients, and our advisory support and profit-share with the FBA.

Making a business out of anti-slavery consulting is not the easiest sell and one that even copped some criticism from a prospect who accused us of trying to profit from slavery, failing to understand our purpose, sacrifices, and the investment we were making.

So, start by equipping your people. Embed ESG in leadership development. Invite employees into the journey. Tell stories. Celebrate wins. Align compensation with impact.

"We're not preparing the road for our children. We're preparing our children for the road."
— Kari Kampakis

Conclusion

What: ESG is more than risk management—it's the essence of modern leadership.

When: When you embed ESG into your operations and relationships...

Then: You unlock agility, resilience, and legacy.

Whether driven by ethics, compliance, or market demand, the sustainability agenda isn't going away. The only question is, *Will we follow—or will we lead?*

From awareness to action

With a sound ESG impact strategy, companies can bridge the gap between producer and consumer, developing empathy with workers like Pablo, whose hardship powers our convenience.

We can build businesses that work *with* governments, academia, and NGOs to develop ecosystems that are agile, conscious, and future-ready.

We can respond to complex global risks like the *AG Neptune* not with apathy, but with the tools and courage to course-correct toward good.

Our work at Unchained Solutions aims to help businesses turn awareness into agency. To connect the dots between boardroom decisions and real-world impact. To ensure that our supply chains honor human dignity, and that our growth is rooted in responsibility.

The time has come for leadership that moves beyond compliance and toward courage, culture, and long-term contribution.

And the time is now.

Stephen

About Dr. Stephen Morse

Dr. Stephen Morse is the CEO of Unchained Solutions Pty Ltd, a Sydney-based social enterprise and certified B-Corp that enables organizations to make a meaningful contribution to the UN Sustainable Development Goals and improve their ESG reporting and CSR commitments. Stephen has over 25 years' experience in entrepreneurial leadership in the not-for-profit and private sectors, both in Australia and overseas. He's a seasoned public speaker, thought leader, author, and strategist, who brings an engaging and refreshing perspective on how industry professionals and business owners can make a positive and lasting impact on people and planet. Stephen obtained his Doctorate in Human Trafficking Intervention through Fuller Theological Seminary, and MBA through University of Technology Sydney. He currently serves on the Advisory Board of the Freedom Business Alliance and chairs the Ethics Committee of the Australasian Supply Chain Institute.

www.unchainedsolutions.com.au

Introducing Marta Pardo, Spain

Get ready to be inspired by a woman who took the driver's seat at just 16. Marta Pardo, born into a motorsport family, has led teams across 21 countries, from Disney to Marriott. With over 30 years of global leadership, she's an award-winning speaker known for her bold vision, service excellence, and unstoppable energy. Affectionately known as The Audacious Vroomer, Marta blends high-performance mindset with real-world leadership.

Fasten your seatbelt. She's here to help you drive forward with purpose.

CHAPTER FOUR

On the Road to Motivation

Ignite, Drive, and Sustain
High-Performance Teams with
the P-ROAD Method

Start Your Engines!

I still remember my first "race." I was 16, stepping in to run my family's service industry business after my father suffered a heart attack and my mother was diagnosed with multiple sclerosis. The engine of responsibility roared into life, and I had to learn fast how to lead, manage, and inspire people twice my age. That moment shaped me, not just as a young woman, but as a future leader who would learn to navigate pressure, chaos, and the weight of responsibility without losing her spark. Years later, I joined the Walt Disney company, first in Orlando at the San Angel Inn Restaurante, and then in Disneyland Paris. There, I worked at reception and then led the Housekeeping Department with responsibility for more than 180 employees. I had just turned 23. That's where I learned the meaning of emotional leadership. Managing that many people from different cultures, backgrounds, and expectations was not just about structure. It was about listening, inspiring, and creating a culture where people showed up.

Later, as general manager in several hotels across France, I learned this: motivation is not a fluffy concept. It's not a TED Talk or a poster on the wall. It's the backbone of performance. If you want happy clients, you need a team that believes in what they're doing.

When I walked into a hotel that had been losing money for three years, where staff morale was at rock bottom, my first act wasn't to change the budget. It was to change the energy. I met with every department, every leader, every frontliner. I didn't ask what was wrong. I asked, "What do you dream of doing here?" Motivation started to return—not with big speeches, but with real conversations.

Leadership is not necessarily just one race, but you do need a race car driver's mentality.

From driving on dusty go-kart tracks as a kid, through years of late-night repairs, relentless training, and fearless turns on ever-faster circuits, you've finally made it here. The big leagues. The track where legends are made. One race. One shot. You tighten your gloves, adjust your helmet, and listen to the hum of your V8 engine vibrating under the seat.

But then something's off.

Your crew isn't looking at you. One is checking his phone. Another's half-listening. The tires are warm, the machine is ready, but your pit team doesn't feel the same fire. And suddenly, you're not a driver. You're a leader with a problem.

Welcome to today's workplace

The race track has changed. So has the race. Since 2020, the rules of motivation have been rewritten. The old models that featured the carrot and stick, the Friday pep talk, or an annual bonus don't rev the engines of modern teams, especially not with Gen Z and late Millennials in the field.

They crave something deeper:

- Purpose – not just pay checks
- Connection – not command
- Real-time leadership – not once-a-year feedback
- Freedom and recognition – not rigid hierarchy

They want to feel like they're not just tightening bolts but building something that moves the world.

What's missing in motivation today?

- Daily ignition – Yearly speeches don't start engines anymore, but real-time connection does. Motivation needs to be built *daily*, in the corridors, in the break rooms, in the check-ins.
- Shared vision – Teams need *meaning*, not just metrics.
- Purpose over profit!

I remember when I reopened a historical hotel in Lyon, I didn't say "Let's hit targets." I said, "Let's become the pride of this city." My team knew we were building a *legacy*.

- **Tailored fuel** – One-size-fits-all leadership stalls performance. Personalization is so important. One of my chefs only came alive during team contests. I let him organize the "Battle of the Breakfast Buffets." Not only did morale soar, but creativity exploded, and our ratings did too.
- **Mental agility** – In a volatile race, resilience and adaptability are survival tools. One morning in Paris, a strike prevented 80% of our staff from being able to get to work. We had 400

guests arriving. I looked at my managers and said: "Let's serve breakfast with our name badges (and titles) off." We did. And we laughed. Resilience is contagious when the leader goes first.

The Types of Engines in Your Team:

- Turbo engines: Your **high-performers**. Quick off the line, high output, but at risk of burnout if over-revved. You need to check their oil weekly, not just their KPIs.

- Diesel engines: The **steady drivers**. Reliable, loyal, but need acknowledgment to keep their rhythm. Give them visibility and they'll surprise you.

- Hybrid engines: Your **creatives**. Flexible, fast-thinking, but allergic to micromanagement. Unconventional thinkers. Give them a side project and they'll transform to the core.

- Electric engines: **Quiet achievers**, but essential. Efficient and consistent, but sensitive to toxic environments. They won't ask for help, but they notice if you don't offer it.

- Rusty engines: **Stalled starters**. Full of untapped potential but need realignment, mentorship, or a reboot. Often misunderstood. Ask them *why* they're stuck before assuming they want out.

The leader's mission:

Before you can win the race, you need to understand the engines under each manager. It's not about pressing the gas harder; it's about learning when to shift, when to support, and when to rebuild. So, how do you read your dashboard and fine-tune your team's machinery?

Let's take that turn now.

The Toolbox to Ignite and Drive Forward

Motivation isn't brute force. It's finesse. It's knowing when to grip the wheel and when to let it glide, when to go full throttle and when to hold back for the curve.

Let's shift gears.

This framework has helped me train leaders, restructure teams, and re-energize organizations in crisis. It's not just a tool; it's a transformation. This **P-ROAD Method** is your GPS to leadership with impact:

P-ROAD = **P**ersonality – **R**esponsibility – **O**pportunity – **A**ttitude – **D**etermination

P-Road Method - Meaning

P
Personality | Performance | Pro-active | Pioneer
Positive | Persuasive

R
Responsibilities | Respect | Recognize | Realistic
Resist

O
Opportunities | Objectives | Optimistic | Original
Organize | Observe

A
Attitude | Authentic | Adaptiable | Analytical
Affiliatioin | Agile

D
Determination | Director | Diplomatic | Discipline
Dymanic | Delegate

1. Personality: Know the engine you're driving

Every team member comes with their own mechanics. Some need autonomy, others need affirmation. Some run best in sprints, others in marathons. Learn to read each person's style like a driver reads a track: Who are your speedsters? Who's overheating? Who needs a pit stop before they break down?

Example: I was coaching a GM in Barcelona who was struggling with turnover. When we mapped his team's personalities, he realized he was managing everyone the same way. We built a profile for each person after identifying who needed clarity, who needed space, and who needed energy. Within three months, performance stabilized.

> *Motivation isn't brute force. It's finesse. It's knowing when to grip the wheel and when to let it glide, when to go full throttle and when to hold back for the curve.*

The revenue manager, for example, was brilliant with numbers and strategy, but emotionally fragile. She needed reassurance, encouragement, and a calm presence around her. Too much pressure or too many check-ins would shake her confidence, but the right balance of autonomy and quiet support helped her shine.

On the other hand, the operations manager thrived on structure. He needed regular updates, weekly check-ins, and clear expectations to feel secure and stay focused.

Leadership is about adjusting your style to each individual, like tuning different cars for different tracks. Same race, different engines. That's what makes a team perform at its best.

2. Responsibility: Hand over the keys

Ownership is fuel.

When people feel genuinely trusted to steer, they don't just execute. They engage, they commit, they innovate. It's the difference between saying, "I need this done," and asking, "You've got this. How do you want to lead it?"

Example: I remember at one hotel I made a bold move by inviting the entire frontline team to rethink how we welcomed our VIP guests. Not just the managers—everyone. The porters, housekeepers, and receptionists knew our guests better than anyone. What came out of it wasn't just a process. It was pride. Performance was faster, more fluid, and filled with intention. Yes, we improved it by 20%, but more importantly, guests felt it. Because the team owned it.

The same thing occurred during a complex turnaround. Instead of handing down a rigid plan, I brought my leads together and asked them to shape the path forward. Watching them take the initiative, challenge each other, and lead from within—that's when the real shifts happened.

> *When people feel seen, heard, and empowered, they rise. When they feel trusted to take the wheel, they drive differently and they care.*

It wasn't *my* vision anymore. It was ours. And when people feel seen, heard, and empowered, they rise. When they feel trusted to take the wheel, they drive differently, and they care.

3. Opportunity: Open new tracks

Nothing drains a driver like a straight road with no turns. People need curves, challenges, and fresh terrain to stay engaged. That's why I believe in giving opportunities, setting new tasks, stretching roles, even letting someone lead a high-stakes meeting. Sometimes it works; sometimes it doesn't.

Example: Once, I offered my reservations manager a dual role, overseeing the housekeeping department alongside her usual duties. She had talent, commitment, and the right mindset, so I believed she could grow into this new track. But after three months, we both saw it wasn't her race. And that's okay.

Because leadership isn't just about offering chances. It's about knowing when to pivot.

That's when I learned something crucial.

Opportunities are like open tracks. Some drivers accelerate; others realize it's not their race. But we never know unless we have the courage to try.

And then, there are the moments when someone *takes off*.

As leaders, we're not here to keep people in their lane. We're here to give them the space to find the right one.

There was this junior member of a team. Julia was noticeably quiet. Easy to overlook. But I saw a spark. So, I gave her the microphone during a key client pitch, no less. We prepped, we rehearsed… and when the moment came, she owned it. Her voice had power. Her presence changed the room. From that day forward, Julia wasn't the same and neither was our team. She was proof that when you bet on potential, transformation happens.

Some people open tracks and bring clarity; others, acceleration.

As leaders, we're not here to keep people in their lane. We're here to give them the space to find the right one.

4. Attitude: Steer the mindset

Motivation doesn't live in mood. It lives in mindset. Build a team that sees obstacles as chicanes to drift through, not walls to crash into. Catch your team doing things right. Celebrate learning, not just results. Reframe failure as "data," not disaster.

Example: When I worked for the Walt Disney Company, I learned a powerful truth: attitude can shape your entire path and even change your whole race.

At Disney, we weren't just employees. We were called "ambassadors" of the brand. From the moment we stepped into the backstage area, we carried a responsibility: every word, every look, every gesture had to reflect the magic of the company. And the first rule was clear: *attitude comes first.*

One of the most striking things I observed was how people with the right mindset were able to transform their trajectory. I saw cast members begin in operational roles and, through their infectious energy and unwavering positivity, rise into leadership positions. Their skills mattered, yes, but it was their attitude that opened doors. Why? Because in an organization built on creating emotion and delivering unforgettable experiences, technical knowledge can be taught... but attitude is contagious. It influences teams, inspires guests, and turns ordinary moments into extraordinary memories.

In one instance, I watched a colleague shift an entire team dynamic just by showing up every day with empathy, enthusiasm, and kindness. Within weeks, the tension in that team dissolved. Productivity increased. Guests noticed. And leadership took note. That colleague? Promoted.

It reminded me that in any race—whether on a track, in a hotel, or on the conference stage—it's not always the fastest or the strongest who wins. Sometimes it's the one who brings the best attitude to the wheel.

Whether you're leading a team, building a business, or simply navigating your own career, never underestimate the silent power of attitude. It's the starting flag for transformation, performance, and trust.

Lead by example.

5. Determination: Finish the Race

Motivation spikes are great. But they fade. What wins races and careers is grit. Determination. It's that relentless decision to keep showing up, no matter the curve.

Example: When I was a manager at the Marriott property in Monaco, Formula 1 week was unlike anything else. For one intense week, our hotel became home to the best pit crews, engineers, strategists, and drivers in the world. Not just luxury guests but precision teams who lived and breathed performance under pressure.

And here's what struck me: it wasn't just about race day. It was about the weeks of micro-adjustments, strategy meetings at 2:00 a.m., and the way they'd dismantle and reassemble a car 10 times in a night to gain one second on the track.

One second.

That's how much determination mattered.

High performance isn't glamorous. It's disciplined.
It's built in the backstage. It's in the tiny decisions, the
daily mindset, the refusal to give up when it gets hard.

We often had to respond to urgent needs like deep-cleaning racing suits overnight, setting up custom laundry protocols, or turning rooms around in record time to meet changing schedules. Every second counted. Every detail mattered. VIP expectations were sky-high. But instead of collapsing under pressure, my team thrived on it. We had prepared. We had trained. But most of all, we were committed to finishing strong, no matter the challenge.

I remember one night, just past midnight, and after a 17-hour shift, one of my team members looked at me and said, *"Marta, tomorrow we do it all again."* And I said, *"Yes. Because this is our race too."*

This experience taught me something that no textbook ever could: high performance isn't glamorous. It's disciplined. It's built in the backstage. It's in the tiny decisions, the daily mindset, the refusal to give up when it gets hard.

That's why I keep a "Hard Wins" wall in my office with framed moments representing projects, events, and team efforts that nearly failed but didn't. They're not just wins. They're proof that we don't quit. We recalibrate. We move forward. We finish the race.

Because leaders don't just set the pace. They show what it means to endure.

This mindset built in the backstage, strengthened by every Hard Win, became the foundation of how I lead. Over time, I realized that determination alone isn't enough; leadership needs direction, clarity, and purpose.

That's when I began to shape my leadership around a clear structure, something I call **the Three Axes of the Steering Wheel**:

- **Leadership style** → How do you drive?
- **Motivational skillset** → How do you fuel others?
- **Customer experience** → Where is the finish line?

P-Road Steering Wheel

Because without direction, even the best engines just burn fuel. And as any race strategist knows, how wisely you use your resources is crucial. That includes your energy, your team's potential, and your leadership focus.

That's why I developed a three-point set of Pit Stop Actions— simple, strategic moves that keep your people aligned, energized, and ready to perform at every turn:

1. Identify your team's engine types.
2. Craft personal "fuel profiles" for each person.
3. Practice micro-motivations: a five-minute check-in can ignite five hours of engagement.

Because sometimes, the most powerful shift doesn't happen at full speed. It happens in the pit lane. That's where real leadership begins. It's not just about speed. It's about strategy, and how smart, bold, and intentional you become.

So, take a breath. Check your mirrors. It's only just beginning.

Ready to take the wheel?

Let's keep driving.

Marta

About Marta Pardo

At 16, **Marta Pardo** was already leading a team. Born into a racing family, she learned early that leadership is about courage, instinct, and direction. With over 30 years of global experience, today she inspires leaders to take the wheel of their lives with boldness, a spirit of service and unstoppable determination.

www.martapardo.com

Introducing Dr Wendy Lee, Malaysia

Ladies and gentlemen, please welcome a trailblazer in personal branding and leadership presence, Dr. Wendy Lee! She's a Certified Speaking Professional, the founder of Chapter One Asia, and the visionary behind the world's first BrandImage™ Institute. An Adjunct Professor at one of Malaysia's top public universities, Dr. Wendy has transformed over 350,000 professionals across 45 countries. Her work empowers CEOs, government leaders, and dynamic entrepreneurs to lead with impact, confidence, and credibility. Get ready to experience her signature blend of science, substance, and style, because when Dr. Wendy takes the stage, presence isn't just taught, it's felt.

CHAPTER FIVE

Leading with Presence

*Aligning Appearance, Body
Language, and Communication
for Maximum Impact*

Why Presence Matters

"Could you tell her without directly telling her?" the managing director asked. *"We'd like to promote her to Regional VP. But she needs to work on her executive presence and leadership branding. After all, she's the face of our company."*

This was shared with me during a one-on-one consulting session with a VP at a foreign bank. It certainly added an interesting twist to my assignment. Tam (not her real name) was clearly great at her job, but the MD didn't want to appear tactless. So now it was up to me to gently help Tam see how her personal brand was holding her back and to guide her toward aligning her image with the leadership role she was meant to step into.

In a perfect world, your work would speak for itself. But we live in a world where perception shapes possibilities. The way you show up—your look, your vibe, your voice—can either open doors or keep them firmly shut. In my work with corporate leaders across Asia and beyond, one truth keeps coming up: presence isn't just a nice-to-have; it's a career accelerator.

I've seen brilliant minds get overlooked simply because they didn't "look the part," and I've seen others soar after a few tweaks to how they present themselves. It's not about changing who you are. It's about making sure the outside matches the excellence within. When that alignment happens, people notice.

According to research published in *Psychological Science*, people make judgments about others' competence, trustworthiness, and likeability within a tenth of a second based on appearance alone (Todorov et al., 2006). That's not a lot of time to prove your worth—unless your presence is already doing the talking. Presence is that unspoken magic that makes people stop, listen, and take you seriously. It's how your appearance, your body language, and your communication style work together to broadcast credibility, inspire trust, and signal your readiness for the next level.

So, let's unpack how you can lead with presence through what you wear, how you move, and what you say. Allow me to walk you through three key dimensions: appearance, body language, and communication style. These elements support your leadership in three essential areas:

1. Building credibility
2. Advancing your career
3. Creating lasting impact

Together, they form a holistic framework for showing up with purpose and power.

Appearance - Your Visual Brand as a Leader
Credibility: Looking the part (before saying a word)

Visual cues significantly influence the viewer's perception of authority and trustworthiness. A Harvard study found that individuals dressed in more formal clothing performed significantly better on cognitive tests and were perceived as more competent (Slepian et al., 2015).

One of my clients, Daniel, a regional manager at a logistics firm, was a smart and hardworking employee. But he kept getting passed over for promotions. The reason? He looked too junior. His wardrobe was casual, baggy, and gave off "still finding myself" vibes. Initially, he was hesitant to change, insisting that jeans and T-shirts were the norm in a logistics firm. After a style upgrade—structured blazers (especially during morning meetings), sleek dress shoes, and darker, richer tones—he started getting noticed. Within eight months, he was promoted.

Another standout story is Dr K., an accomplished academic who had just stepped into a university-wide leadership role. His ideas were groundbreaking, but his wardrobe (ill-fitting khakis, oversized shirt, and tired shoes) made him blend into the background. After a wardrobe intervention, complete with better fitting shirts, sharp blazers and well-fitted trousers, the feedback was positive from both colleagues and students alike.

Whatever your gender, there are some simple rules to elevate your professionalism:

- **Wear strong lines**: Structured blazers, sharp collars, clean cuts. These speak volumes about decisiveness.

- **Dark suits command respect**: Navy, charcoal, black. They scream authority.
- **Details matter**: From your cufflinks to your briefcase, from your earrings to your handbags, polish isn't a luxury—it's leadership.

Career Growth: Dress for the Role You Want

First impressions open doors. And that first glance happens in seconds. Neuroscience tells us our brains are hardwired to process visual stimuli faster than spoken words (Thorpe et al., 1996), meaning your look speaks before you do.

Different leadership contexts demand different dress codes:
- **Boardroom?** Bring out your power suit.
- **Networking event?** Go for smart-casual with personality.
- **Media appearance?** Stick to solid colors and avoid noisy patterns.

I once coached a female executive for a TV interview. We swapped her floral blouse for a bold teal jacket. That small change transformed how people perceived her. She looked confident, focused, and in control.

Then there was Suraya, a rising star in an oil and gas firm. She had the credentials but lacked visual command. Once we aligned her wardrobe with her personal brand—dresses with small prints, sleek silhouettes, statement watches, and neutral color palettes—her career fast-tracked. She later told me, "Changing my wardrobe was one of the best decisions I've ever made!"

Impact: Style as a signature

You can be memorable without saying a word. That's the magic of a signature style. Psychologists call this the "enclothed cognition" effect: what you wear influences not just how others see you, but how you see yourself (Adam & Galinsky, 2012). When you feel powerful, you act powerful.

Some tools you can play with:

Color psychology: Red for power, blue for trust, green for calm.

Consistent grooming: Hair, nails, accessories—it all adds up.

Intentional dressing: Dress not just to *im*press, but to *ex*press.

Think about Steve Jobs. Black turtleneck, jeans. Instantly recognizable. Or Michelle Obama. Always in elegant, bold-colored dresses and well-tailored pieces, understated yet powerful. Her signature style became synonymous with grace, strength, and approachable leadership. Whether bold like Jobs or graceful like Obama, consistency in your visual identity creates lasting impressions.

Now, imagine your own visual identity. What does it say about your leadership?

Body Language—Speaking Before You Speak

According to psychology professor Albert Mehrabian, facial expression contributes up to 55% of communication effectiveness (Mehrabian, 1971). What you do with your body says more than the words coming out of your mouth—especially in high-stakes situations like interviews, negotiations, or boardroom presentations.

Credibility: Confidence in posture

Leadership starts with how you carry yourself. Walk into a room with your shoulders back, chin slightly lifted, and you've already set the stage for success.

I once worked with a client who was a brilliant analyst, but Melanie struggled to get heard in meetings. She slouched, avoided eye contact, and often looked down at her notes. We worked on body alignment, power posing (yes, it works!), and eye contact. When she had to deliver her next presentation, she stood tall and delivered her segment with such poise that even the CEO took notice. From that day on, she wasn't just seen—she was remembered.

Power posing is a term created by social psychologist Amy Cuddy. It became popular after her TED Talk and research at Harvard. Her study showed that holding open, confident body positions for just two minutes can raise levels of testosterone (the confidence hormone) and lower cortisol (the stress hormone). These changes in hormones can make people feel more powerful and perform better in pressure situations. Amy Cuddy says, "Our bodies change our minds, our minds can change our behavior, and our behavior can change our results." Standing like Wonder Woman—feet apart, hands on hips—for two minutes can boost confidence and make you feel more present and self-assured. Even two minutes of this posture can create real psychological effects.

Then there was Ken, a soft-spoken leader in a government agency. His intellect was obvious, but his presence didn't match. With some posture work, strategic use of stillness, and improved eye contact, Ken transformed into a calm leader who commanded the rooms he entered even before he spoke.

Here are a few tips to boost your presence:
- **Mirroring builds trust:** Create connection by subtly matching your listener's posture.
- **No nervous tics:** Fidgeting, swaying, or playing with your hair can make you seem less confident.
- **Claim your space:** Standing tall with your hands visible shows strength and honesty.

Career Growth: Non-verbal assertiveness

Whether it's pitching an idea, managing a tough client, or asking for a raise, how you physically show up can tip the balance.

Take Juliette, for example. She had just stepped into a VP role at a retail conglomerate. Smart and articulate, but during meetings, she tended to clasp her hands tightly and lean back, which made her appear unsure. After we worked on her stance—adding forward-leaning engagement and more intentional hand gestures—something shifted. Her team started leaning in too, both literally and figuratively.

Non-verbal assertiveness is about more than just *looking* confident. It's about actively conveying presence and clarity.

Here are three key components:

1. **Open posture** to signal engagement
2. **Strong stance** (feet shoulder-width apart) for grounding
3. **Steady hand gestures** that emphasize clarity, not confusion

Psychologist Albert Mehrabian's research[1] reveals that only 7% of communication comes from words; the rest comes 38% from tone (the way the words are said) and 55% from body language and facial expression. This means your physical presence matters far more than the words you say.

By refining how you physically show up, you can unlock new levels of leadership, influence, and career growth.

Gravitas: The power of stillness

Great leaders know how to balance calm with charisma.

Gravitas isn't something you can fake; it's born in the pause. The still moment before you respond. The unhurried breath that anchors your confidence.

Zain was a regional director I coached. He used to pace nervously when presenting, his movements betraying his lack of confidence. But once we trained him to stay grounded, use stillness strategically, and lean into the silences, something shifted. His delivery became

1   https://www.businessballs.com/communication-skills/mehrabians-communication-theory-verbal-non-verbal-body-language/

magnetic. One client even said, "When he speaks, I want to hear more." *That's the essence of presence.*

Here's how you can harness that power:

- **Stillness signals strength**: Stop fidgeting. Be intentional with your movements.
- **Expressiveness creates connection**: Smile. Nod. Use micro-expressions to build relatability and warmth.
- **Purposeful pacing**: Walk with direction, not distraction.

Mastering these techniques can transform how others experience your leadership—and more importantly, how you experience it yourself. Gravitas is not just about what you say but how you show up.

Communication Style - Your Leadership Voice
Credibility: Your words build (or break) trust

How you speak—the words, tone, rhythm, and intention—makes or breaks your leadership perception.

Research by TED speaker and sound expert Julian Treasure shows that people trust voices that are deeper, warmer, and slower-paced. In leadership, a strong voice can carry more influence than even the best idea, because *how* something is said often matters more than *what* is said.

Take Farah, for example. She was a department head who always began with, "I might be wrong, but..." We worked on eliminating those qualifiers and reframing her language to be more assertive: "Based on the data, my recommendation is..." The result? Her influence skyrocketed, and she was soon tapped to lead a cross-functional team.

Another example: Anil, a senior IT manager, frequently used fillers like "kinda," "just," and "I feel like." After we helped him eliminate these and refine his messaging into short, impactful phrases, his presence sharpened, and people began quoting him.

There are three important lessons here:

1. **Drop the apologies**: Don't diminish your own voice.
2. **Cut filler words**: They dilute your impact.
3. **Start with strength**: Clear, purposeful language builds instant credibility.

Career Growth: Influence through language

High performers aren't always the ones promoted. Often, it's the ones who can communicate their value.

Cheryl, a COO, used to deliver quarterly reports that were packed with numbers but no soul. We revamped her approach to include one powerful story per report. One quarter, she began with a story about a frontline staff member who turned a frustrated customer into a lifelong advocate, just by listening and solving the issue quickly. That story didn't just illustrate data; it humanized it. Now, she begins with a customer's experience, adds a metaphor, and finishes with the data. Her board engagement scores have never been higher.

Influential language means:

- **Tone variation**: Monotone kills energy.
- **Storytelling**: Anchors abstract concepts in emotion.
- **Audience awareness**: Adjust for cultural, generational, and contextual fit.

Fun fact: A Stanford study found that stories are 22 times more memorable than facts alone (Zak, 2014). If you want your ideas to stick, wrap them in story.

Impact: The power of story and emotion

*Leadership communication isn't about impressing—
it's about connecting.*

At a women-in-leadership summit, I once watched a CEO bring the entire room to tears—not by spouting numbers, but by sharing the story of how her mother's struggles shaped her values. That moment defined the entire event.

- **Vulnerability builds trust**: Share wisely, but don't shy away from being human.

- **Metaphors clarify complexity**: Think "Leadership is like gardening—you don't pull the roots to make things grow."

- **Silence is power**: Use pauses to give your message room to breathe.

Neuroscientist Antonio Damasio discovered that emotions play a critical role in decision-making and memory. His research shows that when the emotional centers of the brain are damaged, people struggle to make even simple decisions (Damasio, 1994). This means that when you tie emotion to your message, it becomes far more memorable and impactful. Make your audiences, customers, colleagues, and communities feel seen, heard, and inspired—because what they feel is what they'll remember.

*"Leadership doesn't begin when you speak. It begins
the moment you are seen, felt, and remembered."*

Align to amplify

When your appearance, body language, and communication align, you step into true leadership presence. It's not about being the loudest, boldest, or most stylish. It's about being intentional. When you look the part, move with purpose, and speak with clarity, people take notice.

Here's your reflection checklist:
- Does your look say "future-ready leader"?
- Is your body language confident and calm?
- Are your words creating impact, not just noise?

Leadership isn't a title. It's an experience you create for others. So go ahead. Raise your game. Refine your presence. Let your leadership speak before you even open your mouth.

Because when you lead with presence, you don't just walk into the room—you own it.

Wendy

About Dr Wendy Lee CSP, CBIP

Dr. Wendy Lee, CSP, is a global image strategist, Adjunct Professor at a top Malaysian university, and founder of Chapter One Asia and the BrandImage™ Institute. She has empowered over 350,000 professionals across 45 countries to lead with polish and purpose. She believes leadership starts with presence—and that a great outfit doesn't hurt, either.

www.linkedin.com/in/drwendylee

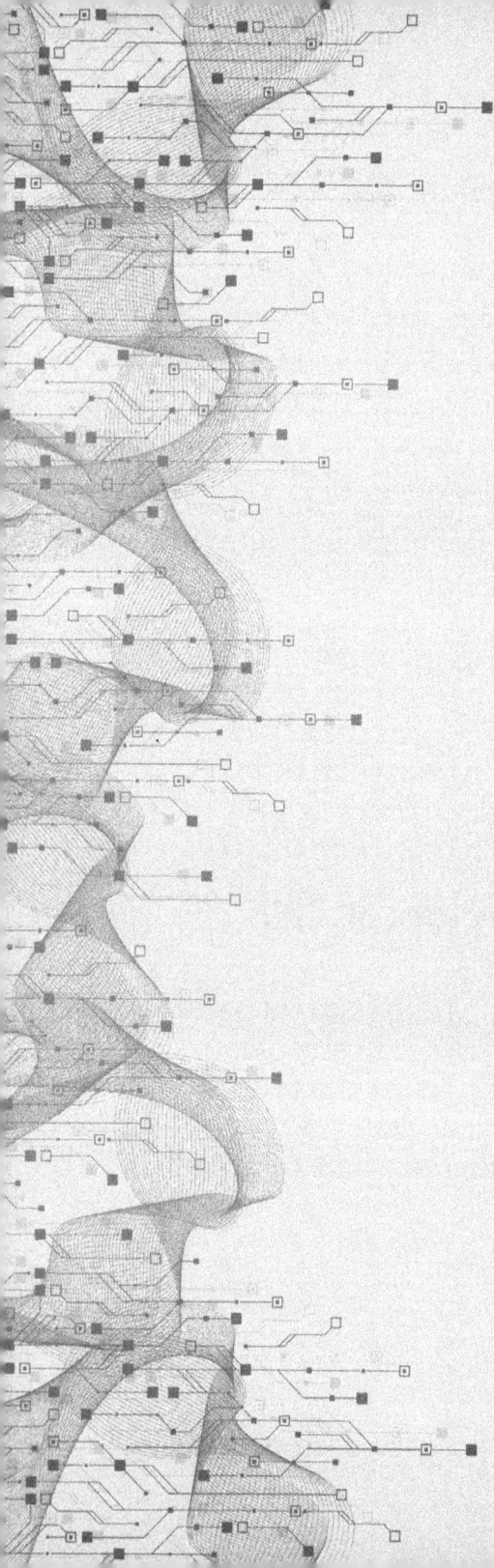

SESSION TWO

Teams

Chantelle Botha
Adrienne Gibson
Nehru Nagappan

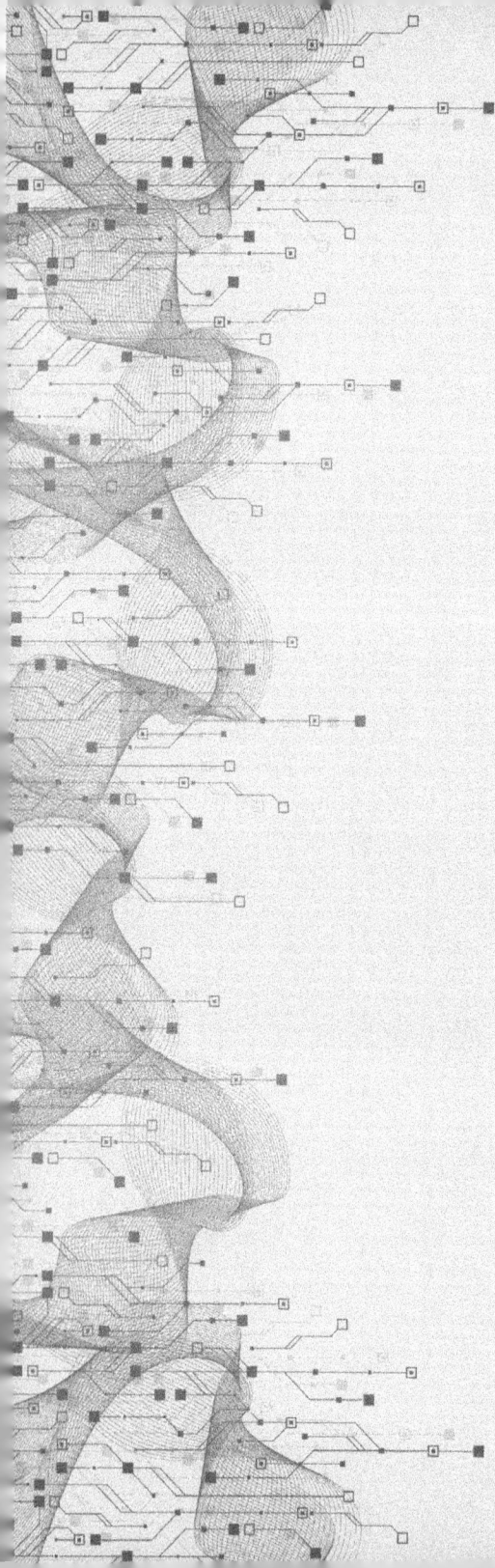

Welcome to the Teams Session

Welcome back to our Connect, Lead, Succeed "Conference in a Book." This session is all about **Teams**—how we build them, lead them, and help them thrive across borders, industries, and cultures.

Kicking things off is **Adrienne Gibson**, a global business transformation leader, whose chapter Navigating Global Cultures tackles one of today's greatest leadership challenges, working across cultural boundaries. With warmth and wisdom, Adrienne shares insights on how diverse teams can thrive when we lead with curiosity, inclusivity, and cultural fluency.

Next, we welcome **Chantelle Botha**, founder of BrandLove and an expert in designing transformative employee experiences. In her chapter, From Bedroom to Boardroom and Beyond, Chantelle brings a refreshingly human take on building connected, engaged teams in a hybrid world. She explores how to create workplaces where people feel valued, inspired, and truly at home.

Finally, **Nehru Nagappan**, leadership mentor and transformation consultant, brings us Creating a Mastermind Group, a powerful reflection on how great leaders don't go it alone. Nehru walks us through how to engage, align, and inspire people through complexity, uncertainty, and change. His message is clear: successful teams are built on trust and shared purpose.

Together, these voices offer essential tools for leaders looking to unlock the full potential of their teams wherever in the world they may be.

Let's dive in.

Introducing Adrienne Gibson, Portugal

Adrienne is an international speaker, coach, and transformation guide with over 30 years of experience leading global change across more than 100 countries. She brings a rare ability to go beneath the surface, uncovering what's unseen but essential in creating real, lasting transformation. With deep insight and a gift for connection, she helps individuals and organizations foster inclusion, engagement, and human-centered leadership across cultures. Adrienne's work blends practical strategy with soulful depth—inviting people into spaces where meaningful change becomes possible.

CHAPTER SIX
Navigating Global Cultures

*Creating Engaging Teams
That Get Results*

I n today's workplaces, teams often include people from varied cultural backgrounds, whether team members are working in the same location or dispersed around the world. With increases in immigration, remote working, outsourcing, and connecting virtually, global business is no longer the exception. It is the norm, making cultural intelligence as important as strategic thinking.

Nowhere has that been more apparent than when I joined a global leadership team tasked with integrating four legacy businesses into one post-acquisition. The acquiring Japanese company was well established with a rich history dating back 200 years. (I'll refer to them as Kaizen for the sake of this example.) In its quest to increase global reach, Kaizen acquired three global companies, two of which were headquartered in the US. The US and Japan… two cultures that could not be more different, as the teams would quickly experience.

By the time I joined, there were already tensions, delays, and frustrations among each of the legacy businesses. Technical leaders representing teams in nearly 50 countries—and each with their own ideas and recommendations—had been gathering for months to discuss options to integrate systems from all four businesses. A technical plan was purportedly progressing, but there were frequent delays, escalations, and disagreements among the team members. Key business stakeholders were growing frustrated with the missed deadlines, conflicting information, and lack of transparency. The pressure was growing for the leadership team to deliver results—and fast!

As timelines passed and tensions rose, finger pointing, blame, criticism, and conflict ramped up. Feedback from local teams on the ground started surfacing. We were hearing things like:

- "They're not listening to us."
- "Why don't they ever speak up or share ideas?"
- "They agreed to what we discussed, but then they didn't follow through."
- "They make changes before we agree to anything."
- "They take forever to do anything. Don't they know this is urgent?"
- "We know this is urgent and are speaking with the team to agree changes; we must get everyone in agreement before we can begin."
- "We can't wait on them forever. Our stakeholders are pressuring us to take action now."

As we peeled back the layers of the feedback, it was clear the teams were operating in legacy silos, using their own approaches and focusing on their own stakeholders rather than operating as one team. The overarching issue, however, was the lack of cross-cultural awareness.

This was more than a difference in ideas, perspectives on recommended solutions, challenges with navigating time zones for global meetings, or misunderstandings in language. The lack of understanding and consideration for cross-cultural dynamics in communicating, exchanging ideas, making decisions, and establishing urgency, as well as conflicting views on authority and hierarchy, were the biggest contributors to the problems the teams were experiencing.

This team was no different to many other global teams around the world. How many times have you heard frustrated leaders, team members, or customers sharing painful cross-cultural experiences? The confusion. The misunderstandings. Apparent agreement stalled, delayed—or worse, cancelled altogether.

If you've ever led a global team, there's no doubt you will have experienced this on some level. And I can guarantee your team members working with others from different cultures are feeling it too. So, what can you do to create more cohesion, collaboration, and performance in your team?

For starters, let's consider what each of us brings to the table when we gather as a team. It's not just our ideas, expertise, education, and work experience. Each of us also brings our own sense of what "correct" looks like in our culture, which has shaped our perspectives on things like:

- **General business etiquette** – what is (and isn't) appropriate in the workplace
- **Feedback and conflict** – how to appropriately challenge each other, give and receive feedback, raise questions or concerns, or handle conflict
- **Hierarchy** – how we defer to or regard leadership, hierarchy, seniority (in age, tenure or position)

- **Decision-making** – who makes the call, and how to confirm agreement
- **Timelines, schedules, and urgency** – what does "on time" or "late" or "urgent" really mean?
- **Relationships and trust** – how trust is built at work and how important relationships are (or aren't) in business.

You likely have a sense of what feels right for you. But someone from a different cultural background will typically have a different view; in some cases, a vastly different view. (An exception to this is people who have lived and worked in several different countries, who tend to have a more blended view rather than operating in extremes.)

Why does this matter?

Because team dynamics and individual and company performance are all impacted by how well (or not so well) we understand, navigate, and consciously create environments that account for the inevitable differences in the way we interact with each other and share work priorities. When cross-cultural awareness is prioritized, people from different nationalities are fully engaged, contributing ideas, aligned on business initiatives and priorities, and performing at levels that produce improved, tangible business outcomes.

Let's explore some strategies for how you can create such an environment.

Don't Make Assumptions

This is the most important strategy for leaders and teams working with those with different cultural backgrounds. In the case of Kaizen, this was one of the biggest fail points among all the teams. The American team members assumed their Japanese colleagues operated with the same perspectives on business.

During regular virtual meetings, the American team members

were accustomed to speaking quickly, sharing their ideas, and questioning each other freely, even talking over or interrupting each other. Their Japanese counterparts found this uncomfortable. In contrast, they allowed someone to finish completely, waiting for a period of time in silence to respect the speaker had completed their thoughts before gently adding their own. As a result of this difference in communication style, the American colleagues would end up speaking for nearly the entire call, leaving no room for the Japanese colleagues to offer their input in a way they felt was respectful and appropriate. This inevitably resulted in feelings of *"they never speak up"* or *"they don't welcome our ideas."*

This same dynamic played out in other areas like making decisions, confirming agreement, and creating a sense of urgency. The Americans expected decisions to be made on the spot during a meeting with whoever was present. Their Japanese colleagues, however, would view the discussions in meetings as topics to discuss with their peers and ultimately their manager, who would formalize the decision once there was agreement from the team. Unaware of this context, the American team members assumed their Japanese colleagues were in agreement simply because they were nodding their heads—a nonverbal acknowledgement which, for the Japanese, meant they *understood*, not that they *agreed*.

Likewise, the sense of urgency meant something different to each group. For the team in Japan, things were moving more rapidly than they were accustomed to. Their approach tended to have a longer-term orientation, taking time to build consensus and explore longer-term impacts of decisions. The American teams were more familiar with getting things done swiftly and were often praised for how fast changes could be implemented. They felt the Japanese side were dragging things out painfully slowly, while *their* key stakeholders escalated complaints, blaming *them* for not moving as quickly as in the past.

The situation was stressful for everyone involved, largely due to the assumptions being made without confirming understanding each other.

How can you avoid this dynamic in your team?

The first step is creating awareness of the potential for making false assumptions.

A best practice is to get to know team members individually, to understand their preferences, ways of working, communication styles, how they raise questions or handle conflict, or their sense of urgency (to name a few). This can be done one-on-one between colleagues or leaders and their team members, or perhaps even as a team-building exercise to elicit input from all team members on their beliefs and preferences. Whatever the method you choose, the key is to create more individual understanding. *Ask, rather than assume!*

Create Clear Team Norms

One of the best investments in any team is to consciously devote time and energy to getting clear about how the team will work together.

This is true whether you have a new team member or leader, a newly established team or project, or even for well-established teams. Creating space to openly discuss ways of working can create a cohesive and collaborative team, which ultimately leads to greater team and company performance.

When working with global teams—and particularly in more diverse teams—mutual understanding can mitigate, or at least reduce, potential conflict, delays, and challenges.

As we saw with Kaizen, in the absence of agreed ways of working together, team members defaulted to their own experiences and preferences, which quickly led to conflict and challenges among the team—not to mention major performance issues and missed deadlines. Conflicts and misunderstandings were repeatedly escalated to the senior leadership team to resolve, which meant our focus was shifted from strategic thinking and keeping stakeholders informed to "firefighting" misunderstandings within our own teams. Our reduced engagement and communication with key stakeholders caused frustration and dissatisfaction for them, which only compounded everyone's problems.

We learned a valuable lesson when we overlooked the importance of first gaining agreement on team norms and ways of working. While it is always best to make such agreements at the beginning, it is worthwhile for teams at any stage, especially when there are conflicting approaches, misalignment on priorities, or changes in team dynamics, like team members or leaders joining or leaving.

Another of the most globally diverse teams I worked with tackled this by gathering together their team members in person to participate in team-building activities to deepen relationships and build more trust. They met on a quarterly basis in different parts of the world to demonstrate respect for where team members were located. Spending a few days together learning about each other's experiences, styles, preferences, priorities and expectations led to outstanding results with increased team engagement, collaboration, and communication. This in turn led to greater alignment, improved performance, consistently meeting deadlines and, ultimately, better operational results and stakeholder satisfaction.

Gathering the team in person, where possible, is the best way to discuss team norms. It also enables more relationship building and connecting, which helps avert potential conflict when team members know each other on a more personal level.

Additionally, language barriers are common in multicultural teams. In-person meetings tend to offer more opportunities to navigate language challenges. This option beats virtual and audio-only every time. Engaging in person means non-verbal forms of communication—facial expressions, body language, and tone—become part of the exchange. (Although, beware: nonverbal communication can also be a source of confusion and misunderstanding, as different cultures view similar gestures and expressions very differently, as pointed out with the Kaizen example earlier.)

While agreeing team norms and ways of working can encompass a wide variety of topics, those that are most helpful in diverse, cross-cultural teams are alignment on how the team will approach:

- Sharing ideas and offering suggestions
- Handling conflict, constructively challenging each other or providing negative feedback
- Priorities, deadlines, and approaches to time/urgency
- Communication methods, including preferences for different methods and styles (in-person; in writing; one-to-one; small or large group, etc.)
- Decision-making and commitments
- Role of the leader vs team member

Following up in writing on what was discussed and agreed also helps overcome language barriers and gives team members the opportunity to *check their understanding* and raise questions for clarity, before things potentially derail from more misunderstandings or misinterpretations. That's a top tip for all meetings where decisions are made or actions required afterwards, especially where team members are not speaking in their own native language.

Regardless of how well team members come to know each other, they may still be hesitant about disclosing "I don't understand what you are saying." Most people are reluctant to raise questions about their peers' accents or pronunciation to avoid embarrassing themselves or their colleague. This is where following up in writing can be a valuable safety net.

Creating team norms won't mitigate all the potential challenges but will certainly get ahead of the majority. It is key to revisit the team norms regularly, to discuss what works and what doesn't, making modifications as needed so the team is continuously improving and evolving their ways of working, performance, and effectiveness. *It's definitely not a once-and-done approach!*

Be Patient and Keep Learning and Refining

*Working across cultures generally takes a bit more
time and requires more patience.*

Beyond the challenges of working around different time zones, there are many elements to cross-cultural dynamics that also demand more patience.

In the Kaizen situation, practicing patience was especially challenging. The teams had widely divergent views on appropriate timelines for making decisions and completing assignments. Attempting to get the American teams to slow down when they were operating at what felt like warp speed to others was difficult, to say the least. It wasn't just the team members; it was also resetting expectations for their stakeholders, who had come to expect rapid turnaround times. Of all the aspects of managing conflicts between the teams, finding the right operational pace was one of the most difficult.

Some of those challenges made perfect sense. For example, when English is a second language for many, dialects, accents, and word choices may make communication more challenging. It is especially difficult to understand others who speak quickly, especially in virtual environments. In-person meetings and written documents helped alleviate those issues, but with Kaizen we needed to go further.

Clearly, speaking more slowly led to better understanding, as did choosing more commonly understood words rather than slang or jargon. While common advice is to not put a lot of words on slides, the opposite holds true in cross-cultural environments. Team members were more likely to understand when they could read along, rather than having to listen to an unfamiliar pronunciation or accent.

Body language was also important to address. Nodding in understanding is different from nodding as a form of agreement. Silence at the end of a speech or crossed arms and firm faces or certain hand gestures might also be easily misunderstood.

Slowing down was more than just communication and word choice. It was also important to allow more time during meetings or discussions for questions and clarification. We also learned it's best to pause often to ask: "What questions do you have so far?" Asking in this manner indicated questions were *expected*, which made it more comfortable for colleagues who were challenged by accents to save face—a cultural imperative of East Asian cultures, like Japan's.

Another element that required more patience was the establishment of trusted relationships among team members. This was, in part, hindered by time zones and the fact that most meetings were virtual. However, beyond that, we recognized how differently cultures approach relationship building. To create a cohesive team, we needed to devote time for team members to get to know each other. This meant gathering in person more often, having social events outside formal settings, and creating space in meetings for *chit chat* and catching up rather than just getting straight down to business.

I was in a position to help team members get to know each other more deeply. It meant they were more patient and understanding with each other, giving each other the benefit of the doubt and remaining willing to discuss things collegially and collaboratively.

It also meant there were fewer escalations to the senior leadership team, which allowed us to focus on more strategic initiatives. This wasn't time wasting; this made a significant difference to how well team members worked together, which translated into improved performance.

Lastly, taking more time to gain agreement on decisions allowed us to ensure we had full buy-in and commitment. To enable this, we circulated ideas for discussion in advance of meetings and allowed extra time for discussions and challenges, as well as time after meetings for team members to gain support locally. It was difficult at times to have the patience needed for the additional time, but the strategy ensured we had the support and commitment needed to move forward. That was a major factor in avoiding subsequent delays and missed deadlines.

We learned the valuable lesson of slowing down early and often or paying the price later.

On the surface, slowing down to allow for clearer communication, prioritizing relationship building, and making timely decisions can seem counterintuitive to getting results. However, taking the time up front to prioritize these aspects creates significant momentum that leads to improved performance outcomes. When meetings or discussions are rushed, it's usually at the cost of something else—like shared understanding, full contribution of ideas, or even something as vital as commitment. We learned the valuable lesson of slowing down early and often—or paying the price later.

Conclusion

Working with team members from different cultures can be incredibly rewarding and interesting when approached with an open mind. Assuming those from other cultures have the same approach to work or that they should follow the culture of the boss is a big mistake.

> *Taking time to get to know team members, their styles and preferences, creating team norms and slowing down to gain agreement and commitment pays tremendous dividends in performance and results later.*

Embodying the spirit of kaizen (a Japanese approach to business that means making continuous improvements or making "good change") enables strong global leaders to continuously learn, adapt, and refine to enhance the experiences of their teams and, ultimately, performance outcomes.

Adrienne

About Adrienne Gibson

An international speaker, coach, and transformation guide, Adrienne enables people and organizations to get to the heart of what's holding people or systems back and create lasting change. With decades of experience across 100+ countries, she blends deep insight with practical tools to foster connection, inclusion, and meaningful transformation in life and business.

www.adriennegibson.com

Introducing Chantelle Botha, South Africa

She's not just a speaker; she's a spark that sets transformation alight. An international power-house known for igniting confidence through identity architecture, Chantelle takes us on a journey from the bedroom to the boardroom—and far beyond. Unapologetically authentic, with piercing insight, she shows how the deepest truths about who we are shape how we lead, connect, and succeed. Founder of Phoenix and author of Phoenix Rising, she's here to crack open comfort zones and call us into courageous connection. Buckle up—because Chantelle doesn't just speak... she recalibrates.

CHAPTER SEVEN

Bedroom to Boardroom & Beyond

The quality of our lives depends on the quality of our relationships. Whether we're building careers, families, or partnerships, relationships are the foundation and the fiber. They shape everything we create... or fail to create.

How we relate in the bedroom, the boardroom, and beyond determines the trajectory of our lives. Yet for too long, we've kept this truth in the shadows. It's time to bring it into the light.

The longest-running scientific study on happiness and well-being (the Harvard Study of Adult Development, ongoing since 1938), makes it clear: the single greatest predictor of long-term happiness and health is strong, supportive relationships.

And yet, something doesn't add up.

According to O.C. Tanner's 2024 Global Culture Report, 80% of workers feel overlooked and underappreciated. Why? Lack of trust, fear of conflict, and weak commitment—classic symptoms of team dysfunction, as outlined by Patrick Lencioni. And dysfunction doesn't just cost us productivity. It erodes culture, breeds disengagement, and fuels the epidemic of "quiet quitting."

Technology hasn't helped. We check our phones an average of 85 times a day and feel more disconnected than ever. Communication skills, once core to leadership, are deteriorating. Not just in the workplace, but in our most intimate relationships too.

Daniel is a brilliant finance manager. Reliable. A perfectionist. He always gets the job done. But if you ask anyone on his team what he's really thinking, they wouldn't know. Daniel doesn't speak up in meetings unless he's asked directly. He avoids conflict, never gives feedback, and when a misunderstanding happens, he just lets it simmer rather than addressing it.

His director says, "He's too reserved." His colleagues say, "He's hard to read." But the truth is… Daniel is scared of being misunderstood. Or worse—rejected.

So where did it come from?

Daniel's identity as a communicator—or rather, a non-communicator—wasn't shaped in the boardroom. It was shaped in the bedroom, long before he entered the workforce.

For years, Daniel was in a relationship where communication about intimacy was laced with shame and silence. Whenever he tried to express a desire, a need, or even confusion, he was met with deflection, discomfort, or worse—stonewalling. Over time, he learned that vulnerability made things worse, not better. His words felt like weapons that backfired.

So he shut down.

He stopped asking for what he needed. He learned to anticipate others, over-function, and avoid the risk of rejection by never rocking the boat. The bedroom became a training ground in self-silencing. He didn't realize it at the time, but it bled into every other relationship, especially work.

Now, in the office, Daniel avoids hard conversations. He withholds ideas until they're perfect. He feels anxious when feedback is given and apologizes even when it's not his fault. He doesn't realize it, but his identity has become "The less I say, the safer I am."

But the silence is costing him. Promotions pass him by. His team sees him as distant. And his potential? It's stuck behind a wall of protection he built years ago in the most vulnerable place of all—the bedroom.

The Identity Crisis Behind Communication Problems

If Daniel's story resonates with us—if we recognize we have a Daniel inside us—isn't it time we rewrote the story? We don't have communication problems; we have a crisis of *identity*.

Leaders and teams today are grappling not just with tasks and targets but with a disconnection from *themselves*. We're bombarded with digital noise—often including contentious conversations about gender and personal identity—and societal pressure about who we should be. Authenticity is talked about but rarely lived.

Mental health statistics reflect the toll: anxiety and depression affect one in four people, with economic impacts projected in the trillions. In my coaching work with global leaders, the game changer isn't productivity hacks. It's identity integrity. At the heart of it, we're longing to be seen. Identity isn't personal. It's the foundation of connection, culture, and success.

When people reconnect with who they really are, communication flows naturally. Teams shift. Cultures shift. One client, a supervisor at PepsiCo, came to me for time management support. But through identity-focused coaching, she discovered her struggle was really about boundaries and self-worth. The result? Within three months, she won two company awards, one for saving her division over $50,000 a month.

> *If we want better communication, better teams, and better results, we have to start at the core:* **Who am I?**

If we want better communication, better teams, and better results, we have to start at the core: *Who am I?* Because once that's clear, everything else becomes easier to say—and hear.

Sanet, a senior director, noticed that what she communicated vs what her team heard were two different things. She initiated a discovery process and faced her sense of isolation and disconnect from her authentic self for the first time. As she built up her identity, she noticed that she was more confident in speaking up at work and more secure in trusting her communications.

Within months, she introduced reflective exercises to her team and saw the subtle shift in how they started showing up. Eventually, I delivered a talk to her team—this time, about ditching ego and building lasting, meaningful relationships. The result? Team meetings that once felt like monologues became open, curious conversations.

Team identity, like personal identity, is an ever-evolving thing, and we need to remember to allow room for change and growth as we solidify our understanding of who we are individually as well as collectively.

The Deeper Layers of Identity in Leadership

Identity is more than a job title or personality trait. It's the full spectrum of roles, values, beliefs, goals, and life experiences that shape how we show up in the world. At its core, identity sets the ceiling for our potential. We rarely outperform our internal self-image.

I have developed a seven-layer identity map, where each layer logically builds upon the previous one—from external to internal, conscious to subconscious—and helps people connect the dots between their *outer performance* and their *inner programming*:

1. Surface-level roles and titles that inform how we are perceived by our peers and, ultimately, the results we get in work and life.

2. Talents, skills, and capabilities—the things that lead us to our roles and titles.

3. Values and principles guide what matters to us. These are shaped by our core beliefs, and they express themselves through our talents and capabilities.

4. Emotions—we can either express or repress our emotions. Regulated expression of our emotions feeds into our values and capabilities, while repression feeds into warped beliefs that play out in increasingly unproductive behavior.

5. Core beliefs about self and world which inform the stories we tell ourselves about why things happen the way they do—these stories play out in our emotions.

6. Formative experiences from our culture and upbringing that solidify our beliefs and shape our behavior.

7. Unprocessed experiences (the shadow self), which we may not even be aware of, yet which create our core beliefs.

For many high achievers, that shadow includes a belief of not being good enough. The result? A workaholic pattern that seems like success on the surface but stems from unresolved trauma beneath.

Carl Jung said, "Until you make the unconscious conscious, it will rule your life and you will call it fate." Our unacknowledged beliefs not only shape careers but deeply influence personal connection and self-worth. One area where this unconscious shaping is especially potent—but often overlooked—is our sexual identity.

The Whole-Person Approach

An essential part of identity that often goes unaddressed is our relationship with our bodies and, by extension, our sexuality. Sexuality isn't just about what we do; it's central to *who we are*. When we disconnect from that part of ourselves, we mute confidence, communication, and authenticity. Yet society tells us to suppress it. Sexual education often focuses on abstinence and risk avoidance. The rest we learn from media, pornography, or painful trial and error. This disconnect breeds shame, anxiety, and disconnection.

The National Sexual Violence Resource Center reports that 81% of women and 43% of men have experienced sexual harassment or assault. Whether through direct trauma or cultural shame, many people are uncomfortable with sexuality. Unsurprisingly, this filters into work. When we fear judgment or repress a part of ourselves, our communication suffers and our leadership becomes inauthentic.

"Whoa, Chantelle, are you telling me we need to discuss our sexuality around the boardroom table?!"

No… of course not! What I am advocating for is accepting our sexuality as a foundational component of our identity. The more work we do on discovering and shaping our identities, the closer we will sail to accepting ourselves as whole people.

In my own journey, chronic disconnect from my physical and

sexual identity led to four decades of anxiety, depression, and low confidence. In *Phoenix Rising*, I explore how reconnection with my body and pleasure shifted everything—including my performance as a leader.

Ali Abdaal, in *Feel Good Productivity*, shows that we work better when we feel good. Pleasure matters. It rewires our brains and makes us more engaged, creative, and connected. My group coaching clients consistently experience greater confidence at work after embracing their sensual and sexual selves.

The power of sexual identity

If you can't speak up in the bedroom, how can you fully speak up in a boardroom? If you feel shame about who you are behind closed doors, how can you challenge the status quo in leadership?

Boundary-setting is another critical skill that transfers across all areas of life. We learn how to communicate boundaries in the bedroom, and this extends to how we communicate boundaries in the boardroom. Boundary violations are, in essence, consent violations.

Renee felt like she was drowning in an ever-growing pile of deliverables at work. She constantly said yes, even when her plate was full, afraid of disappointing others or seeming incapable.

I challenged her to ask her husband for *exactly* what she wanted during intimacy. It felt awkward at first. After all, their sex life seemed fine. But within a few weeks, something shifted. Their connection deepened. She felt heard, seen, respected.

And then something clicked. She carried that confidence into work. Renee scheduled a meeting with key stakeholders and unapologetically communicated what she could and couldn't deliver. The result? Respect. Clarity. Space to breathe.

By learning to voice her desires in the bedroom, she gave herself permission to speak up in the boardroom.

That's the power of integrated identity—being the same authentic self across every domain of life. And it's transformational for leadership and teams.

Sexual identity is the blueprint for how we show up in teams, in relationships, in life. As Napoleon Hill acknowledged in *Think and Grow Rich*, sexual energy is a powerful creative force. What better place to channel some of that energy than into meaningful, purposeful work?

He's not the only one to have written about the power of sexual energy. Sigmund Freud explored human sexuality's impact on behavior and psychology, and Carl Jung discussed the concept of *anima and animus*, emphasizing the balance of masculine and feminine energies within individuals. Wilhelm Reich advanced the idea of "*orgone energy*," viewing sexual energy as vital for health and well-being and arguing for its liberating power. David Deida, a contemporary author and speaker, connects sexual energy to spirituality and personal growth, particularly in the context of relationships.

Now more than ever, there's a call to come home to your whole self. Identity work is not just personal—it's professional. It's the difference between surviving and thriving in leadership.

The Evolution of Identity in Leadership

Personal identity is not static; it evolves as we do. Crafting it is less about labels and more about deep discovery. Tamara, an executive head of product development, fully committed to this process. As she peeled back years of conditioning, she found her core truth. She went from "*I AM*"—owning her identity—to "*I CAN*," as her confidence grew. That became "*I DO*," as she acted from authenticity, and finally "*I LEAD*," stepping into a bigger role and now completing her doctorate in business leadership. This is the power of identity work.

But what happens when we skip the root cause and slap a Band-Aid on the symptoms? More skills training. More tools. No change.

We need to go deeper.

Some time back, I turned a potential client away. Being a "training junkie," he thought he could cure his inability to achieve executive status through ever more courses and certifications. He told a sad tale of being passed over time and again, even though his qualifications far outranked those of his peers who advanced their careers.

His frustration was palpable! He asked me for the playbook—the actual steps in the strategy that would achieve his goal.

I explained that before we could implement strategy, the first step would be to accept that he was responsible for his stagnation. The chip on his shoulder needed healing before he could create the relationships that would unlock the next opportunity.

Unfortunately, he was blinded by a victim mentality. Refusing to accept responsibility for his future and choosing instead to blame others, I told him I could not work with him. All the training in the world wouldn't help until he addressed his identity issues.

The simplicity of identity-based solutions

In an identity-based workshop for new recruits at one of South Africa's leading banks, every participant reported how basic embodiment practices—like breathing, grounding, and self-awareness—helped them focus and perform better.

This simple intervention had a profound impact. The success of that pilot sparked discussions to expand the program, this time including long-term support and accountability.

---

*Why did it work? Because how we **see** ourselves determines how we **show up**, and how we show up dictates the results we get.*

Most communication issues in teams are not about skills gaps. They're symptoms of a deeper disease: disconnection. From self. From others. From purpose. When identity is unexamined and the body is ignored, we can't bring our full selves to the table.

The historical context of connection

To understand what's at risk in our increasingly disconnected workplaces, let's look back. Early humans formed tribes for survival—shared vision, task division, mutual protection. Disagreements existed, of course, but reconciling was necessary. Exile meant death.

As society evolved through the agricultural and industrial ages, we used both mind and body to build community and progress.

Then came the information age. Technology became our problem solver, addressing poverty, disease, and violence. While it has improved lives, it's also fractured our sense of belonging. We've replaced tight-knit tribes with digital networks, leaving people lonelier than ever. We compete for attention on global platforms, and even those who "win" often feel anxious, insecure, and disconnected. We crave genuine connection but settle for curated online validation.

The risk of disembodiment

Technology has not increased the amount of human attention available. It has only amplified both the best and worst in us.

Futurists like Charlotte Kemp and Graeme Codrington speak of disruption, adaptability, and preparing for what's ahead. Kemp highlights two intersecting forces shaping our world: *scarcity vs. abundance* and *binary vs. fluid*. Without intentional adaptation, she warns, success—even survival—will be out of reach.

What's missing from their dialogue is embodiment and its potential to preface connection. As we advance through the digital era, our bodies are becoming increasingly irrelevant. In past eras, we needed our bodies to farm, build, or move. Now, most of us sit behind screens, working with our minds alone. We've become "knowledge workers," but we've forgotten that the mind is housed in the body.

We are becoming disembodied.

AI is accelerating this disconnection. It helps us increase productivity, even filling gaps in mental health care. But if machines start to meet all our needs, practical and emotional, what happens to our humanity? At what point will we stop noticing our craving for real, flesh-and-blood connection?

The Warning Signs of Cultural Collapse

This isn't just about loneliness; it's a warning sign of cultural collapse. When we lose connection to ourselves, we lose connection to others. Over time, we lose what makes us human.

When we lose connection to ourselves, we lose connection to others. Over time, we lose what makes us human.

Historian Arnold Toynbee studied the rise and fall of 28 civilizations. His conclusion? *"Civilizations die from suicide, not by murder."*

Are we doing the same?

Eastern philosophies have long embraced the mind-body connection. Now, some Western leaders are beginning to follow suit by returning to presence, mindfulness, and embodiment. It's not complicated. But in our rush to find complex solutions, we often overlook the simplest: reconnection with the body.

The path forward

The world is crying out for workplaces where people are valued as whole humans. It's not enough to develop talent. We must also cultivate authenticity.

We are flesh, blood, and brain—not algorithms. We are wired for connection, and yes, for pleasure. Physical, emotional, intellectual. What happens in our bodies shapes what happens in our minds. They are not separate.

To build dynamic teams and resilient cultures, we must start by reclaiming our humanity. That means integrating all aspects of ourselves—even the ones we're taught to hide. From the boardroom to the bedroom, from ambition to emotion, from intellect to intuition.

We cannot keep numbing, fragmenting, and bypassing who we truly are.

The call is simple but urgent. Reconnect:

- With yourself—all parts of yourself
- With your team—beyond titles and functions
- With your purpose—the deeper why behind your work

This reconnection begins with identity integrity. When you understand who you truly are, communication flows, leadership strengthens, and teams thrive.

And isn't that what we all want? To connect, lead, and succeed—as our full, authentic selves.

I help teams do just that, starting with the individual. Ready to begin?

Chantelle

About Chantelle Botha

Chantelle Botha, The Catalyst, helps leaders unlock magnetic confidence by integrating identity and embodiment. An international speaker, coach, and founder of Phoenix, she transforms communication by bridging boardroom performance with personal authenticity. Her mission: to ignite unapologetic self-expression that fuels deep connection, impactful leadership, and sustainable success.

www.phoenixconfidence.com

Introducing Nehru Nagappan, Malaysia

Nehru Nagappan is a seasoned project management and PMO expert and a global strategist with 36 years of experience across multiple industries and regions. As founder of MyPMGenie, he has trained over 47,000 professionals in project management and leadership. Nehru has managed high-profile projects such as The Walt Disney in Hong Kong and has been an advisor to many GLC/government organizations. He holds numerous certifications, including PMP and CB-PMO, and has served on the Board of Directors at the Project Management Institute, PMO Global Institute, and other professional organizations. He is well known for his dynamic, fun, and engaging speaking style.

CHAPTER EIGHT
Creating a Mastermind Group

Unleashing Collective Power

With decades of experience leading high-impact projects—from Hong Kong Disneyland to major government initiatives—I've seen how solo brilliance can stall. Mastermind groups, by contrast, unlock collective intelligence and fast-track breakthroughs. This chapter offers a practical framework often missing from typical team dynamics and leadership discussions, focused on real-world collaboration.

Emma sank into her chair as the afternoon glow slanted across her desk. She had marched through more slide decks and data deep-dives than she could count yet still felt stuck. Her startup's next big milestone eluded her; each solo brainstorming session ended in another loop of half-formed ideas. She'd even tried a "power hour," blocking off 60 minutes to think uninterrupted. Instead, she found herself staring at the same blank slide, her confidence eroding with every passing minute. Doubt whispered: "Maybe I don't have what it takes."

That afternoon, she invited five trusted colleagues into her sunlit conference room:

- Ana from product design
- Marcus from finance
- Priya from operations
- Leo on sales strategy
- An old competitor-turned-mentor, Rafael

Emma half-expected polite updates and cautious nods. Instead, the room crackled to life. A flippant comment about customer churn ignited a debate on tiered pricing. Marcus sketched a quick revenue chart that uncovered an overlooked upsell opportunity. Priya spotted a process bottleneck that, once resolved, freed up critical resources. By session's end, Emma held a roadmap so clear it pulsed in her fingertips and felt destined to succeed.

In the 1930s, Dr Napoleon Hill introduced the "Master Mind" concept, where minds in harmony create a powerful "third force" beyond individual capacity. Today, research confirms that well-structured groups outperform individuals. This synergy—what I call the "Spark Field"—is a leader's edge: a focused circle accelerating collective breakthroughs and innovation. Leadership legends today don't just emerge from solitary genius; they arise from thoughtfully curated circles.

Emma's breakthrough mirrored this modern playbook. Minutes into her two-hour session, she realized her problem wasn't complexity. It was her perspective. Alone, she'd fixated on marketing tactics; in a group, she saw how pricing, customer feedback, and operational flow intertwined. Within a week, her team implemented the revised plan. A month later, trial sign-ups jumped 15%, and her quarterly growth outpaced projections by 10%.

This Spark Field ignites only when you curate your circle intentionally. Aim for four to eight participants. Fewer than four risks tunnel vision; more than eight fragments the discussion and buries quieter voices. Each person is like an instrument: a solo violin is lovely, but a quartet's harmony gives it real power.

Why size matters:

- Focus: A tight group keeps conversations centered on your core challenge, avoiding sidebar debates.
- Engagement: Everyone has airtime; no one fades into the background.
- Practicality: Coordinating eight calendars is doable; any more becomes a logistical headache. Groups larger than 8–10 members lose cohesion and focus. Smaller circles (4–6) foster deeper dialogue and personal accountability.

Modern leaders in practice:

- I recently worked with a social-enterprise founder to help them convene five advisors—from marketing to community outreach—to revamp a fundraising campaign. Their combined insights inspired a peer-to-peer giving model that boosted donations by 40%.
- At a fast-growing app company I consulted to, the leadership team gathered six specialists in finance, customer support, and product design, and two external thought-partners. Their monthly sessions halved release cycles by identifying potential roadblocks before they became crises.

Each of these circles was lean, purposeful, and rooted in mutual accountability. By aligning varied expertise around a single challenge, they unlocked solutions more quickly and elegantly than any individual strategist could.

Before diving in, picture your own Emma moment and the clarity and momentum that emerge when isolation ends and fresh perspectives align. This chapter shows you how to build that Spark Field: selecting the right people, busting common myths, setting clear purpose, and embedding rituals that transform you from solo thinker to collaborative leader.

Dispelling the Myths That Stifle Your Circle

When Emma first set out to build her Spark Field, she stumbled straight into some classic traps. Let's follow her journey as she learns to dismantle these myths and, in the process, keeps her circle vibrant and forward-moving.

Myth 1: "More Voices = More Value"

Emma's first mastermind attempt included her entire leadership team—12 people from sales, marketing, finance, customer support, and beyond. She pictured a hive of buzzing ideas, but what she got was chaos. Side conversations splintered the group, and quieter contributors drifted to the margins. Frustrated, Emma realized bigger wasn't better.

Emma's pivot: She relaunched with just six carefully chosen peers. In that tighter circle, Ana's design critique found space to breathe, Priya's operations insight landed fully, and Marcus's revenue sketch sparked a viable upsell strategy.

Reflection: Who truly needs a seat at your table—and who might be more effective in a one-on-one deep dive?

Myth 2: "A Big Name Guarantees Big Impact"

Next, Emma thought a high-profile consultant would elevate her group. He joined with fanfare, but offered only broad platitudes and showed up late, treating sessions like another calendar obligation. His prestige overshadowed genuine contribution, and Emma's Spark Field dimmed once more.

Emma's pivot: She refocused her invites on peers with burning challenges tied to her North Star. When she asked each candidate, "What one problem do you wake up thinking about?", the energy in her calls returned, and so did the depth of ideas in her meetings.

Reflection: In your invitations, frame the ask around specific challenges, not resumes or titles.

Myth 3: Harmony Equals Progress

On her third try, Emma assembled a small, enthusiastic group, but everyone was too polite to challenge one another. Their plans felt safe but uninspired, and no real breakthroughs emerged.

Emma's pivot: She introduced a rotating *provocateur* role. In the next session, Leo played devil's advocate, asking, "What if our customers hate this feature?" Suddenly, hidden flaws surfaced, and the group reworked their approach into something significantly stronger.

Reflection: Who in your circle can take on the role of constructive challenger, and how will you prepare them?

Myth 4: Frequent Meetings Guarantee Momentum

Eager to maintain traction, Emma tried weekly 90-minute calls. But by the third week, enthusiasm waned. Updates felt redundant, and members began to skip sessions.

Emma's pivot: She shifted to a 90-minute deep dive once a month, with optional 30-minute "hot seat" check-ins for urgent blockers. Attendance climbed back to 100%, and each session felt fresh and high-impact.

Reflection: What meeting rhythm might preserve your circle's energy while keeping you on track?

Myth 5: Free-Form Equals Freedom

In pursuit of spontaneity, Emma once scrapped agendas entirely.

Two hours later, the group had generated plenty of ideas, but none were ready to implement.

Emma's pivot: She began sending a one-question pre-work prompt 48 hours before meetings: "What's the single obstacle you need us to solve?"

That focused everyone's preparation and transformed their two hours together into a crucible for actionable solutions.

Reflection: What pre-work question will prime your members for the most meaningful breakthroughs?

By learning from Emma's missteps and implementing these pivots, you'll cultivate a lean, enthusiastic circle of four to eight peers, each fully engaged, constructively challenging, and committed to your shared North Star. By busting these five myths, you'll strip away the hidden barriers that sap the mastermind energy. Instead, you'll create a lean, hungry circle of four to eight committed peers, united in purpose and primed to spark each other's best thinking.

Hand-Picking Your Dream Circle

When Emma first sent out invitations for her Spark Field experiment, she cast a wide net: her marketing director, an external consultant she admired, two product managers, and a junior analyst whose voice she wanted to encourage. On paper, it looked perfect—a spectrum of roles and seniorities. Yet, at that kick-off, the group never quite gelled. The consultant kept steering discussions toward high-level theory, the junior analyst barely spoke, and the product managers fell into technical jargon. Emma realized she'd traded one form of isolation for another: she was back to nodding politely as voices clashed without harmony.

That misstep taught Emma a vital lesson: curation matters more than coverage. To hand-pick a truly transformative circle, she adopted a four-step process, one you can follow in your own leadership journey.

Sharpen your core challenge

Emma returned to the blank slide deck and distilled her aim into a single sentence: "I need to increase our product's trial-to-paying conversion by 20% within three months."

That crystal-clear focus became her North Star, guiding every decision about whom to invite.

As you jot down your North Star, encapsulate your core challenge in one sentence. Place it at the top of a fresh document. This is your circle's rallying cry.

Map the perspectives you lack

With her North Star in hand, Emma listed missing viewpoints: customer psychology, pricing strategy, onboarding experience, and fresh market intelligence. She prioritized recruits who could fill those gaps, rather than gathering everyone who held a seat at the table.

As you jot down your North Star, on the same document, write down three to five areas where you feel least confident. Beside each, note a role or industry that could supply insight (e.g., pricing strategist, behavioral psychologist, industry outsider).

Vet for passion over position

In her next round of invites, Emma replaced the unnamed consultant with a start-up founder who had lived her exact challenge and burned nights crafting subscription models. On discovery calls, she asked: "What one obstacle keeps you up at 2 a.m.?"

She focused less on polished credentials and looked for more fire in their eyes. Those who spoke in abstract generalities bowed out; those who described specific, angst-driven problems leaned in.

Seal the commitment with clarity

Once Emma had five enthusiastic "yes" replies, she sent a concise welcome packet:

- Their shared North Star
- The 90-minute monthly timebox, defended like a board-level meeting
- Three ground rules: strict confidentiality, punctuality, and ownership of commitments

She ended with one ask: "Reply 'I'm in' by this Friday, and we're official."

That simple act aligned expectations and built collective energy from day one.

As you jot down your North Star, create your welcome packet outline including timebox details and three non-negotiables. Keep it to one page and ask for a clear "I'm in" response.

Try Emma's four-step approach: nail your challenge, find the perspectives you lack, recruit for fire over title, and seal the deal clearly. You'll end up with a circle built for spark.

How do you transform that group into a living blueprint for breakthroughs, ensuring every meeting drives measurable progress?

From Blueprint to Breakthroughs

A charter is only as good as the behaviors it encourages. Emma reminded the group that their charter wasn't a static document sitting on a shelf. It would guide every email, every agenda, and every follow-up. She introduced two simple yet powerful techniques to embed the blueprint:

- **Charter reminders:** At the top of every email invite and meeting slide deck, the North Star and top metric are displayed in a banner—constant visual anchors that realign focus.
- **Metric moments:** At the close of each session, Emma

reviews the agreed-upon metrics, tracking progress with a quick dashboard. Seeing the percentage of completed actions tick upward on screen became a mini celebration in itself.

Within two cycles, the group had locked down 10 key decisions, completed 88% of their action items, and reported an average confidence score of 4.2. What began as abstract ambition had become measurable success.

Craft your charter

Before your next meeting, follow Emma's co-creation steps:

1. **North Star scrapbook:** Invite members to write their purpose sentences on virtual sticky notes. Cluster and refine into one rallying cry.

2. **Metric matching:** Propose five potential success markers. Debate pros and cons, then vote on your top three.

3. **Meeting blueprint:** Draft an agenda flow that balances deep dives with quick pivots. Test and tweak based on your first session's energy.

4. By co-creating your blueprint, you transform it from a dry plan into a living roadmap, one that every member has shaped and now champions.

Sustaining your momentum

By their third meeting—six weeks after launching—the energy in Emma's circle threatened to wane. Initial excitement had given way to competing deadlines, and one member even missed a session. Determined to preserve their Spark Field, Emma introduced a suite of rituals and tools that embedded the mastermind into everyone's leadership routine.

Honor the rhythm with timeboxing

Emma treated their 90-minute monthly session as inviolable. She blocked it on calendars six months in advance and began each meeting with a clear countdown timer, starting and ending strictly on the dot. Borrowing from Agile, this **timeboxing** insured against tangents and respected every member's schedule. The result: laser-focused discussions and zero meeting fatigue.

Rotate the helm with support

After two sessions, Emma handed the facilitator's baton to Priya. To ensure a smooth transition, she shared a one-page **facilitation cheat-sheet**, detailing agenda flow, timing cues, and prompts like "Pause for reflection" or "Invite a quieter voice." Priya co-facilitated first with Emma as her co-pilot, then ran a session solo. The group's confidence in each other's leadership grew, and so did their collective trust.

Pair up for accountability

Between meetings, Emma paired members as accountability buddies, but she didn't stop there. She layered in two more tactics:

1. **Public progress board:** In their shared project workspace, each member logged monthly commitments alongside a simple color coded status indicator: Not Started, In Progress, or Done. Visibility drove follow-through. No one wanted their action lingering in red.

2. **Micro-challenge check-ins:** Mid-cycle, Emma posted a quick two-question poll ("Rate your progress 1–5" and "What's one barrier right now?"), sparking problem-solving threads and preventing small obstacles from becoming roadblocks.

Together, these rituals lifted on-time completion rates to over 90%.

Celebrate micro-wins

Emma kicked off each meeting with a two-minute **Victory Lap**, where members shared even tiny successes, like securing a pilot partner or refining a slide deck. To make these moments stick, she introduced a simple tech tip: a shared "Win" channel in their team chat app, where anyone could drop kudos or screenshots of progress anytime. That ongoing digital applause kept morale high between sessions.

Tune up and refresh

Every six months, Emma led a **Circle Retrospective**: revisiting their North Star, reviewing success metrics, and collecting anonymous feedback on what worked and what needed tweaking. This biannual check-in ensured the charter evolved with their goals—sometimes adding a new member, other times refining a metric to stay aligned with shifting priorities.

Thanks to these sustaining practices, Emma's Spark Field didn't fizzle. It blazed brighter. Their circle became an unshakable engine of growth, driving Emma's product conversion up 25% in 90 days and forging bonds that outlasted any single project.

Nehru

About Nehru Nagappan

Nehru Nagappan, founder of MyPMGenie, is a global project management strategist with decades of cross-industry experience. He has trained over 47,000 professionals and led iconic projects like Hong Kong Disneyland. Renowned for his dynamic style, Nehru advises governments and holds top industry certifications and leadership rolcs.

His training and consultancy programs can be found at *www.mypmgenie.com*

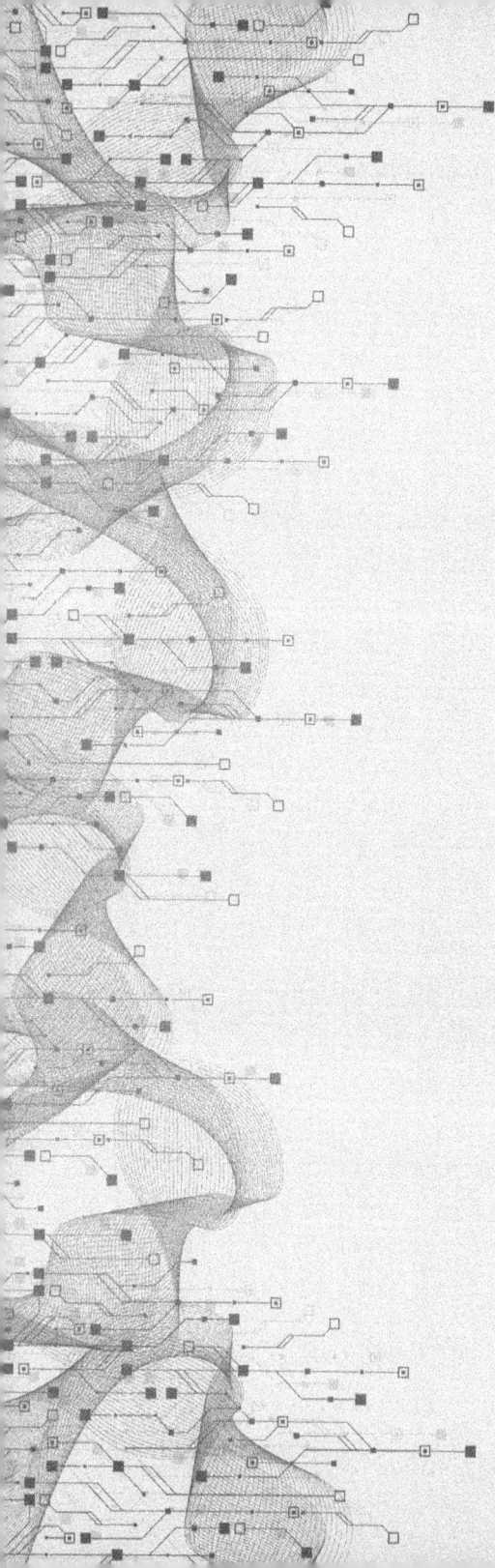

SESSION THREE

Artificial Intelligence (AI)

Fiona Kearns

Liz Hardwick

Nick Sinanan

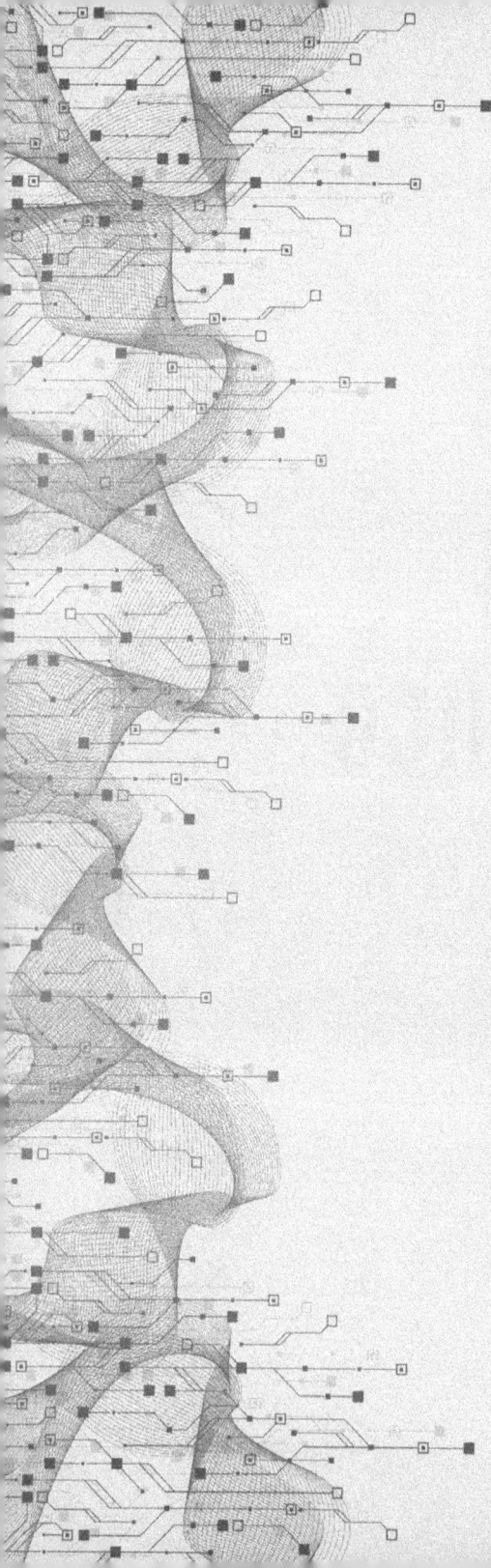

Welcome to the AI Session

Welcome to the AI session of *Connect, Lead, Succeed*—where the future isn't just arriving, it's already integrating into how we think, lead, and communicate.

This isn't about robots taking over. This is about how we, as business leaders, can harness technology to connect more meaningfully, work more intelligently, and lead with clarity in the digital age. In this session, we spotlight three bold thinkers who are bridging the gap between people and machines—with humanity at the heart of it all.

First up is **Fiona Kearns**, with her chapter about AI-Ready leaders and having confidence in a data-driven world. Fiona tackles the mindset shift required to lead with confidence amid uncertainty—unpacking how to stay visible, decisive, and human when data is everywhere and the pressure is high.

Next, **Liz Hardwick** brings us some top tips and strategic ways to work smarter in the AI age. With her signature clarity and tech-savvy charm, Liz shares practical ways to embrace AI tools for productivity, balance, and brilliance—especially for business owners and teams juggling competing demands.

Rounding out the session, **Nick Sinanan** invites us to explore some of ethics of using AI. Nick makes it clear: adapting to AI isn't optional. He lays out a compelling vision of how emotional intelligence, ethics, and strategic awareness are essential tools for any leader ready to thrive in an AI-enhanced world.

This session is your invitation to explore not just the tools but also the thinking required to lead in the age of AI.

Let's begin.

Introducing Fiona Kearns, UK

Get ready for an inspiring and thought-provoking session on Leveraging AI for Success! Please welcome Fiona Kearns, certified business psychologist, former tech CEO, and leadership expert for high-growth businesses. With deep experience across IT, telecoms, and commercial sectors, Fiona combines psychological insight with real-world business acumen. She cuts through the noise to explore how leaders can engage with AI confidently and effectively. In this keynote, she'll share practical strategies to help you lead with clarity, curiosity, and impact in an AI-driven world. If you're ready to think critically, act decisively, and leverage AI for lasting success, this session is for you.

CHAPTER NINE

Leveraging AI for Success

*AI for Automation, Productivity
and Communication*

Pain Point: Fast World - Let AI Help!

In today's digital era, speed is everything. We expect quick answers, rapid results, and instant impact, and we demand quality too. At the same time, the sheer volume of information at our fingertips is overwhelming. While it might seem like the more information the better, the reality is different: more often means slower, more confused, and less effective.

> *AI should be treated as a set of useful tools—not threats—to enhance communication, leadership, and productivity in **real-world**, non-techy environments.*

With the world moving faster every day, leaders must be decisive, strategic, and agile. But with so much noise, how do we cut through to make better decisions, communicate effectively, and truly lead? The answer lies in smart use of technology, and AI can be a powerful ally to help you lead and communicate more effectively. AI enables us to make informed, data-driven decisions faster, helping us stay sharp and impactful both online and offline.

Pain Point: The State of Your Communication is the State of Your Leadership

Leadership and communication are inseparable. For millennia, scholars and strategists have debated what makes a great leader, but most agree on one thing: great leaders are great communicators. Your leadership effectiveness is strongly tied to the quality of your interpersonal skills. Yet, a gap often exists between the leader we aspire to be and how we actually show up in our interactions.

When stress rises and demands increase, communication often suffers. We talk more, listen less, and unintentionally diminish collaboration. But what if AI could help you become more mindful of your communication habits and improve them in real time?

Speak less, lead more

Recognizing imbalance is the first step toward improvement. True leadership communication isn't about speaking more or louder; it's about listening with intention. Leaders who excel at active listening build stronger relationships, uncover better ideas, and drive stronger results.

One simple but powerful measure of communication effectiveness is speaking balance. In healthy conversations—whether in team meetings, one-on-ones, or sales discussions—there should be a natural flow where all voices are heard. When one person dominates, important opportunities for collaboration, learning, and engagement are often lost. In sales, for example, if the seller does most of the talking, it's often a sign the customer's needs are being overlooked. Similarly, if a leader monopolizes a meeting, the team's insights and ownership are diminished.

Becoming aware of how much you're speaking and how much space you're giving others is essential for effective leadership. Fortunately, AI tools can now monitor speaking time in real time during meetings, offering leaders an invaluable window into their communication patterns.

AI can serve as a personal communication coach, providing objective feedback on your speaking habits. By tracking your patterns over time, you can see tangible improvements—not just in how much you speak, but in how meaningfully you connect with others.

Imagine leaving a meeting not *guessing* how you performed, but *knowing*, backed by data that you led an inclusive, engaging conversation.

Managing people remains one of the greatest challenges in leadership. But by using AI-powered speaking-time trackers during online meetings, leaders gain a strategic advantage: the ability to quickly spot imbalances, empower quieter voices, and create a more balanced, inclusive dialogue that drives better outcomes.

Top Tip: Aim to speak less than 40%

These AI tools track speaking time during meetings, raising awareness of communication dynamics. *Be warned: the pop-ups can be distracting!*

- **EmotionIQ** – Analyzes emotional tone in conversations in real time.
- **Participation and Speaker Time Tracker** – Highlights speaking balance to create more inclusive meetings and shares report after the session finishes.

Both tools allow leaders to be more mindful, creating better conversations and stronger teams without waiting for subjective feedback.

Case Study: Course Correction for a Busy Manager

Jack, a high-performing manager under constant pressure, realized he was slipping into a directive, "telling" style of leadership. By using an AI conversation-tracking tool, Jack saw that he dominated meetings far more than he realized. This insight allowed him to course-correct, embracing a more coaching-oriented style where his team members spoke more and took greater ownership.

The result? Better ideas, greater engagement, and improved performance. Jack believes this simple AI feedback has been transformational, not only in virtual meetings but also in face-to-face conversations.

Personal Reflection: Fiona's Favorites

As someone who loves to engage and share, I found these tools incredibly helpful for self-regulation. Instead of relying on external feedback, the data spoke for itself. I could adjust my speaking habits, and that resulted in better, more productive conversations both online and offline.

By bringing AI into our leadership toolbox, we're not replacing human connection. We're enhancing it. Mindful, data-supported communication is the future of great leadership.

Learning Enhancement and Information Management with AI

Real World Pain Point: Drowning in Data – How AI Helps You Sail Smoothly.

Email inboxes are a perfect symbol of how overwhelmed professionals feel today. Despite all the productivity hacks we try, email, which was meant to save us time, often just adds to the stress. It is estimated we are hit with an average of 121 emails and 226 work-related messages each day. Step away for a while, and the dread of returning to an even bigger mountain of tasks sets in.

Managing all this information is no longer just about working *harder*. It is about working *smarter*. Like taming your inbox, we need a way to deal with the tidal wave of meetings, reports, and data. Done right, access to all this information should free us. But too often, it leaves us stuck. AI can be a brilliant partner in helping us sort, simplify, and make better decisions.

Being savvy: managing the overwhelm

It is easy to get swept up in the AI hype. You will hear promises that it can do everything, from making your tea to running your business. The truth is many of these fancy tools are not that easy to set up and can leave you feeling even more confused.

According to McKinsey, the management consulting firm, employees spend nearly two hours a day just searching for information. Getting savvy about how we handle information is absolutely critical. Not every shiny new tool will help you. Staying focused on what actually makes a difference is the real trick.

New technology is wonderful, but it must solve real problems first. AI is no different. It has endless possibilities, but the real value comes when it helps you do your job better, not just when it impresses you.

A Personal Story: Technology Meets Practicality

I have always sat somewhere between technology and people. I am not a classic techie, but I have spent my career surrounded by innovation. Back in the early 2000s, I worked at a VoIP (Voice over Internet Protocol) start-up, when the idea of remote working was just getting started.

We had all kinds of exciting features to sell, but ultimately, most customers simply wanted one thing: to make and receive phone calls reliably. That taught me something important. New technology is wonderful, but it must solve real problems first. AI is no different. It has endless possibilities, but the real value comes when it helps you do your job better, not just when it impresses you.

AI can write a song, and my nine-year-old loved doing that at school, but for a business leader, that is not the best use of your time. You do not need to try every tool that comes along. It makes much more sense to focus on improving the systems you already use. Look for ways AI can boost your productivity, improve communication, and give you better insights, rather than chasing the latest trend.

Optimistic *and* reality based: be open to change but not a slave to it!

It is important to be open to change but even more important to stay grounded. I have two examples from my own attempts with AI tools in 2025.

First, I tried setting up a system that would text me whenever an important email arrived. Perfect for when I was away from my inbox for a while. Sadly, it turned out that the service did not work properly in the UK. A real disappointment.

Second, I tried to get ChatGPT and Zapier to work together to draft replies to my emails automatically. Although everything connected correctly, the feature just did not deliver. I spent far too much time fiddling with it before giving up. Maybe it was user error, but either way, it was not worth the effort.

Sometimes, even when the technology looks amazing, it does not fit your needs. You need to use your judgement. Be open to experimenting, but do not let every new tool dictate how you work.

Be open to experimenting, but do not let every new tool dictate how you work.

Practical AI use for leaders

The smartest way to use AI is to get more out of the tools you already rely on. Becoming an advanced user of platforms like Outlook, Teams, or Google Workspace can have a bigger impact than buying into every new piece of software that pops up.

AI tools like ChatGPT or Microsoft Co-pilot can save you time writing emails, creating documents, or summarizing information. You stay in control, polishing and finishing the work.

Other practical uses include:

- Uploading files to AI platforms and asking smart questions
- Analyzing contracts and reports for key issues
- Extracting useful text from images
- Asking for feedback on your own writing

You can even automate tasks using platforms like Zapier but keep it simple. Make sure new tools genuinely fit your work and don't add another layer of complexity.

FIONA'S FAVOURITES:

ChatGPT Gen AI Tool: Search Engine on Steroids

ChatGPT is a fantastic all-round gen AI tool. It's great when you want innovative ways to write important emails, get starter ideas for a project or go deep into a particular subject. It's a paid for tool which you can customize to your own preference such as tone of voice. It's like a search engine on steroids. However, as Abraham Lincoln never said, "Don't believe everything you read on the internet." Be careful of ChatGPT filling in gaps that are "good guesses" but wrong. You need to fact-check the information it provides for you; don't assume its correct. Otherwise, you risk badly damaging your reputation.

Fathom AI: Meeting Note Taker

Fathom AI for meetings is a tool that joins the meeting as a participant. It listens to the meeting and then provides meeting minutes including 'next steps' by email after the session. It provides a good solid summary but may require tweaks. As a free tool, it is very useful and you can pause the recording mid-session if there are topics you don't wish to be included in the notes.

Email Clients: Delayed Sending Function

Email platforms like Google and Outlook let you schedule messages to be sent at a time that suits you. This is especially handy if you work irregular hours, want your email to land when it's most convenient for the reader, or prefer to manage expectations by not replying too quickly. Outlook even offers an option to delay every email by one minute—perfect for anyone who tends to notice mistakes just after hitting 'send'. For those people, it's a real game changer.

Neurodiversity and Inclusivity Support
Pain Point: Poor Systems Limit Potential of our Neurospicy Team Members

Embracing neurodiversity does more than foster a sense of belonging; it offers a strategic advantage. By creating environments that welcome different ways of thinking, organizations can tap into exceptional skills, creativity, and problem-solving abilities that neurodivergent colleagues bring. Artificial Intelligence is emerging as a critical ally in this effort, offering tools that make communication, information sharing, and task management more inclusive and accessible.

AI-driven accessibility tools are transforming how we support neurodivergent professionals. Real-time captioning features in Zoom, Microsoft Teams, and PowerPoint can make meetings and presentations more inclusive by offering instant subtitles. This can be helpful for individuals who process auditory information differently or need visual reinforcement to focus better.

For example, PowerPoint's real-time subtitle functionality not only improves accessibility during live presentations but also ensures that key points are captured for later review. Testing and refining these tools further can perfect their ability to meet the needs of diverse audiences, ensuring that no team member feels left out of the conversation.

Personally, I love a good subtitle—and it gives me the freedom to not have earphones!

AI also offers new ways to share information. Text summarizer, visual content generators, and text-to-speech systems allow individuals to consume material in the format that best suits their cognitive preferences. A dense report can become a set of visual slides or a brief audio summary, enabling better comprehension and retention for neurodivergent team members.

Ava's Story

Ava was a project manager with ADHD. Traditional scheduling tools often overwhelmed her with a flood of deadlines and reminders. However, with the help of an AI-assisted scheduling tool that prioritized and structured her tasks visually, Ava thrived. The AI did not replace her need for structure; it amplified her ability to manage it in a way that fit her brain's rhythm.

Beyond scheduling, structured planners, grammar assistants, and tone-checking tools help professionals fine-tune their communication. AI can suggest more organized ways to present ideas, correct minor errors in real time, and even flag when a message's tone might be misinterpreted. For those with dyslexia, autism, or ADHD, these small supports can significantly boost confidence and effectiveness.

Moreover, AI's ability to create visual aids, organize tasks dynamically, and adjust communication styles according to individual needs positions it as an essential companion for inclusive leadership.

- Time management apps powered by AI can offer gentle nudges instead of overwhelming alerts.
- Error-correction tools can discreetly enhance clarity in communication.
- Real-time feedback can help individuals course-correct without fear of judgement.

Embracing neurodiversity with the help of AI tools is not merely a matter of compliance or goodwill; it is a profound investment in the strength and resilience of the organization itself.

The broader takeaway is clear: AI can serve as a powerful equalizer and accessibility champion. When thoughtfully deployed, it ensures that everyone, not just the neurotypical majority, can contribute fully and comfortably. Importantly, leveraging AI to support neurodiversity does not mean replacing empathy with algorithms. Instead, it is about using technology to *enhance* empathy, creating a workplace where every individual's way of working is respected and empowered.

Embracing neurodiversity with the help of AI tools is not merely a matter of compliance or goodwill; it is a profound investment in the strength and resilience of the organization itself.

Here are two things you can do immediately to further embrace how AI can enhance your leadership style.

Tool overwhelm and focus: Choose just two or three key AI tools and focus on mastering them, rather than trying to learn them all.

In-person networking angle: Decide how AI can enhance your *offline* leadership and relationships (e.g., pre-meeting prep, emotion tracking).

AI can definitely help leaders cut through the noise and focus on what matters. But it only works if you stay practical and selective. Use AI to build on what you already do well. Be willing to try new things but stay firmly in the driver's seat. Technology should work for you, not the other way around.

Fiona

About Fiona Kearns

Fiona Kearns, certified business psychologist and former tech CEO, works across IT, non-profit and commercial sectors to build leadership capability for investment and growth. With a strong IT background, she brings a critical, practical perspective on AI's workplace impact, supporting clients to lead effectively in a fast-changing technological landscape.

www.kearnsconsultancy.com/ai

Introducing Liz Hardwick, UK

In a world buzzing with AI hype, today's speaker brings something refreshingly rare… clarity. Liz Hardwick CSP is a globally recognized voice in digital productivity, known for turning tech overwhelm into smart, sustainable action. With over 25 years in the digital sector, she empowers business leaders to navigate change with confidence, curiosity, and a people-first mindset. Whether guiding teams through AI integration or sparking lightbulb moments on stage, Liz leaves audiences inspired and equipped. Get ready for insights you'll want to take back to your own teams…

Please welcome, Liz Hardwick!

CHAPTER TEN

Harnessing AI for Productivity

Practical Strategies for Business Owners and Leaders

In today's digital world, business owners and leaders face constant pressure to stay ahead. Artificial Intelligence (AI) promises to boost productivity, streamline operations, and drive smarter decision-making. Used intentionally, AI doesn't just help us keep up; it can help us see what's next and prepare for the future, too. However, time and time again, I see businesses wasting valuable time and energy on generic, one-size-fits-all solutions, usually because they haven't had the right training or dedicated the time to learning the tools properly. The real opportunity lies not in chasing every shiny new tool (I know it's hard not to!) but in developing a tailored, strategic approach to integrating AI across your goals, workflows, and teams.

As a global speaker, trainer, and productivity specialist with over 20 years in the digital sector, I help leaders and their teams embrace digital tools in a way that improves outcomes and preserves well-being. My approach is always practical and real-world focused. I believe AI shouldn't be exhausting... it should be empowering!

In this chapter, I'll share with you how you can integrate AI with existing workflows, enhance time management techniques, and speed up content creation for people-first productivity. Beyond just efficiency, I'll highlight how harnessing AI is a great form of transferring knowledge and skills too, helping businesses stay ahead of the curve and spot the "what's next?" opportunities in their industries.

This chapter will focus on creating lasting impact—long after the latest AI hot-topic has gone cold—with actionable strategies to prepare yourself for a future that balances innovation, productivity, and growth with the irreplaceable human touch that makes your business unique.

Why AI Belongs in Your Business Toolkit
Rewriting the rulebook: What AI really is and why it matters

At its core, AI refers to systems that simulate human intelligence to perform tasks such as understanding language, recognizing patterns or making decisions. While the term often conjures images of robots and science fiction, the reality is more grounded... and more useful.

In my keynote talks on AI and digital tools for boosting productivity, I share that AI can offer enhanced productivity, smarter resource allocation, and innovation at scale. From email sorting to customer insights and content generation, AI can already perform many repetitive or time-consuming tasks faster and more consistently than humans. But there are concerns, too, from data protection and ethical decision-making to fears around job displacement and the future of human labor.

> *The goal isn't to replace humans with machines but to empower people to do more of the work only they can do.*

Rather than ignoring these complexities, we need to face them head on, engaging with unions, regulators, and our own teams. The goal isn't to replace humans with machines but to empower people to do more of the work only they can do.

Having worked with trade unions for over 10 years on their digital training, I can tell you that AI is now their favourite topic in conversations, questions, and concerns. When engaging with them about this, my top suggestion on how to have a harmonized workplace is to position AI as a *supportive* force rather than a *disruptive* one. Bring your people with you on the journey from concept and testing to implementation. These approaches not only minimize resistance, but they also open new avenues for staff development, upskilling and cross-skilling, and long-term engagement. Inviting employees to be a key part of the technological evolution invites a growth mindset into the business culture that displaces fear.

The most forward-thinking companies I work with aren't waiting for perfection. They're experimenting, measuring outcomes, and creating a roadmap that evolves. As AI becomes increasingly embedded in everyday tools and systems, this mindset becomes a key competitive advantage.

AI should be empowering, not exhausting

The real magic of AI lies in its ability to be personalized. Business owners and entrepreneurs often dabble with popular tools mentioned in the media like ChatGPT or Midjourney, and then walk away underwhelmed.

Why? Because they're using generic prompts, disconnected tools, and no clear strategy.

To truly harness AI, we need to move beyond the basics. That could mean developing a chatbot specifically tailored to your business FAQs, using a customized scheduling assistant that understands your preferred meeting patterns, or implementing an AI tool that reviews and suggests improvements to your weekly reports. It's about aligning the tools with your goals.

Imagine your team using an AI dashboard that highlights priority tasks for the week based on project goals and past performance trends. Or a sales leader receiving AI-generated summaries of customer feedback that allow them to make quicker, smarter adjustments. These examples show that AI, when configured well, reduces stress rather than exacerbates it.

AI isn't just a timesaver. It's a clarity booster when the goal is not just to automate but to amplify.

When used correctly, it can help surface insights that humans might miss, highlight emerging risks, and identify opportunities faster than traditional methods. From sentiment analysis in customer service to trend tracking in marketing, the goal is not just to automate but to amplify.

This shift also involves re-learning *how to learn*. The digital world is moving fast, and I encourage leaders to stay curious, open, and willing to experiment. Your AI setup should feel like a virtual teammate… not another thing on your to-do list!

Humans at the heart: Why AI needs us

There's a misconception that AI is here to take over humans. However, the most effective systems are those where humans and technology complement each other. AI excels at analyzing data, identifying patterns, and automating repetitive work. But empathy, creativity, innovation, and leadership remain uniquely human skills.

(Try asking ChatGPT how they feel for more of an insight!)

One powerful example I often use is in recruitment. Sure, AI can help filter CVs based on key criteria, but only a human can assess cultural fit, team chemistry, or emotional intelligence. The best AI-powered systems are those that *support* decision-making without removing human nuance.

> *AI should supplement human work, not replace it. The companies that thrive are the ones that strategically blend talent and tech, creating roles that evolve, rather than disappear.*

The same is true in areas like negotiation, coaching, and innovation. AI can assist with background research or generate talking points, but we human beings remain essential for building trust and relationships.

By freeing up time spent on admin (and the tasks we don't like), we can give our teams space to lead, create, and connect. AI should supplement human work, not replace it. The companies that thrive are the ones that strategically blend talent and tech, creating roles that evolve, rather than disappear.

I always encourage businesses to view AI as an enabler of people, not a substitute. This mindset shift makes it easier to adopt any kind of new technology without fear and ensures AI is aligned with human-centered values.

How Businesses are Actually Using AI Today
Hidden AI: The AI tools already in your workflow

AI might already be supporting your business, even if you haven't realized it. Tools like Zoom and Microsoft Teams use AI to improve background noise reduction, automate meeting transcriptions, and even suggest follow-up tasks. Canva's Magic Write AI feature drafts marketing copy in seconds and Grammarly uses AI to refine professional communication, all using AI as a tool within their systems.

Even email clients are joining the movement. Google Workspace and Microsoft Outlook now offer smart replies, predictive typing, and priority inbox sorting, all powered by AI. These time-saving nudges often go unnoticed but are already changing how we communicate and manage our time.

Another under-the-radar helper I love to recommend is Otter.ai, which provides live transcription and summaries of meetings and interviews. This supports accessibility and boosts efficiency for those who learn best visually or need post-meeting clarity.

We normally only use 36% of any software or tool features, so by identifying the hidden helpers you already have access to, you can explore how to use them more intentionally or build on them with additional tools for deeper results.

Small, strategic changes like this can snowball into wider digital transformation across teams.

Integrated AI for real-world wins

Let's take a look at how businesses are achieving real productivity gains:

1. Smarter time management: Using AI-driven assistants like Motion or Reclaim.ai, teams are automating calendar scheduling, adjusting time blocks based on workload, and protecting focus hours.

One of my VIP productivity coaching clients now saves, on average, eight hours per week in their meeting prep time by using AI-suggested meeting briefs and then tweaking accordingly.

2. Content creation made easy: Once I showcase the bespoke examples, business leaders love using NLP (Natural Language Processing) bots like Jasper or ChatGPT to generate drafts of LinkedIn posts, newsletters, product descriptions, and reports. With some investment of time to create and teach your new bot your voice, brand, preferences, topics, and special blueprints, you can save hours per piece created.

One entrepreneur I support recently cut down their online posting creation time for LinkedIn using a combination of her VA, AI, and scheduling options within LinkedIn. This reduced the time required for tasks associated with this key marketing tool from about four hours to only one hour per week. Now the bulk of her engagement with LinkedIn is to do the human-only part of engaging with comments and personalized relationship touchpoints, as well and proofreading her AI content and making sure her human-ness and brand still shine through.

3. End-to-end workflows: As a global professional speaker, I get very excited by live-translated conferences. At a recent European conference in Belfast, Ireland, the team impressed me with their new Talent and Tech setup. They were running live audio translations for speakers and delegates in eight different languages simultaneously. The organizers understood the value of using human translators and previously hired them to be on-site, sitting in hot sound booths at the side of the hall for days on end. This time, by integrating AI tools, Zoom, and AV technology into their workflow, the conference was managed and translated remotely in real time. Translators worked from their homes across the world, saving countless hours in travel and setup, and allowing organizers to book high-demand translators with greater flexibility. The live translators' audio was then summarized using AI, providing quick recaps in the different languages. It was a brilliant example of combining the best of human skill and smart tech for a seamless experience.

These examples show how AI isn't a standalone solution. It works best when woven into systems people already use. Using AI goes beyond mere efficiency to the creation of a more intuitive, responsive organization that evolves with its people.

Productive AI: Automate the boring, celebrate the brilliant

AI shines when used for the mundane. Think inbox management, data entry, follow-up reminders, or invoice processing. These tasks are consistent, rules-based, and ripe for automation.

This doesn't mean the end of roles for humans who action these tasks; it means evolving them. A marketing assistant who used to spend hours sourcing stock images, resizing graphics, and drafting social media captions can now use AI to generate visual assets and tailored copy in minutes. This frees them up to focus on campaign strategy, audience engagement, and creative direction, which require more human insight and flair.

Retailers are using AI for stock management and demand forecasting. In customer service, chatbots handle initial FAQs while human agents focus on complex queries. In HR, AI supports training compliance, leaving teams free to focus on learning strategy.

The productivity gains are real, but the human outcomes are just as important.

Even in creative fields, AI can help brainstorm ideas, draft scripts, outline campaigns, or visualize ideas, supporting people to bring the boldest ideas to life.

The productivity gains are real, but the human outcomes are just as important. Job satisfaction rises when we're freed from repetitive tasks. And businesses benefit from a balance between speed and soul.

Making AI Work for You
Don't fall for shiny tools: Start with a strategy

With new AI tools launching almost daily, it's easy to get distracted. But real results come from strategic integration, not novelty.

Start by reviewing your current tech-stack.

Here's some questions from my Digital Review Tool...

- What tools do you and your team use every day?
- Where are the friction points or bottlenecks?
- What are you paying for and not using, and—maybe more importantly—why?
- What would you love to have, and need to have, to streamline your business?

You might also find it helpful to visualize your current workflows and identify tasks that are repetitive, time-consuming, prone to human error, or you really just don't want to do.

Then ask yourself: Can AI—or indeed, any kind of digital tool support—streamline or eliminate these pain points? This doesn't always mean buying something new. Sometimes it's about unlocking features you already have at your fingertips.

My digital review process, developed from years of supporting organizations through digital change, helps leaders see the whole picture before jumping in. I guide clients through mapping their ecosystem, highlighting where tools overlap, where there's friction, and where new AI integrations might make a measurable difference.

Keeping on Top in 15 Minutes a Week

Worried about falling behind? Staying AI-savvy needn't take hours.

I recommend setting aside just 15 minutes a week to read one article, explore one new tool, or attend a short webinar. Follow industry voices on LinkedIn or subscribe to RSS news feeds (I love *Feedly* to keep all my news in one place). Build your confidence through small, consistent learning sprints.

I've also worked with teams to set up "Learning Lunches" where staff take turns sharing for 5–15 minutes about something useful they've found, seen, or tested. This builds a learning culture and keeps everyone curious and adaptable.

Over time, these tiny habits build real confidence and spark fresh ideas you can act on right away. Staying current doesn't mean mastering every app. It means building the awareness to ask, "Could this work?"

Your AI roadmap: Build. Test. Adapt. Repeat.

AI integration isn't a one-off project; it's an evolving journey.

I always recommend a test-and-learn mindset.

Choose one area of your workflow to optimize at a time. Look at the tools you already use, find an AI resource that complements them and test it for 90 days. Set clear objectives, get team feedback, and track progress.

Then, review. What worked? What didn't? What could be even better?

You might find some tools work better for certain teams or tasks. That's normal. The goal isn't uniformity; it's usefulness. Use what works, tweak what doesn't, and always focus on real-world impact.

And… repeat.

AI trends may come and go, but the strategies you build today will support sustainable, human-centered productivity for years to come. Creating an AI-enhanced workflow doesn't require perfection. It starts with clear intentions, a willingness to experiment, and a mindset of continuous learning.

When we combine human smarts with the right digital tools, we create space for both efficiency and creativity to thrive. Whether you're leading a corporate team, scaling a fast-growing business, or guiding digital transformation in a membership organization, the message is the same: AI can work for you when it's grounded in purpose and people!

Real productivity isn't just about ticking off tasks and having the latest tech. It's about progress that feels empowering, sustainable, and aligned with what matters most.

Liz

About Liz Hardwick

Liz Hardwick CSP is an award-winning professional speaker, trainer, and entrepreneur, with over 25 years' experience in "harnessing digital for human benefit". She regularly speaks internationally on AI, digital productivity, and focus and time management. Liz has been recognized in TechWomen100 and TechWorld's Top 111 UK Women in Tech Speakers. Make sure you check out the free downloadable resources at:

www.productivityclub.co.uk/ai-for-leaders

Introducing Nick Sinanan, UAE

All right, everyone, buckle up because this keynote is about to blow your mind!

We're diving into "The Double Meaning of Beyond Gen AI"—a roadmap to future-proof leadership and legacy.

Our speaker, a trailblazer who evolved as a parent and AI advocate, has figured out how to merge heart with cutting-edge data. From smarter, faster decisions to harnessing emotional intelligence, mentorship, and next-gen innovation, get ready to learn how to lead with both heart and data.

This is the ultimate fusion of tech and humanity that's reshaping how we build tomorrow's legacy.

Let's jump in!

CHAPTER ELEVEN

The Double Meaning of "Beyond Gen AI"

*The Future of Leadership
and Legacy*

"Artificial Intelligence is the pen with which we are now writing the next chapter of human history." —
Satya Nadella, CEO of Microsoft

We're in the middle of an AI revolution that's completely rewriting leadership and legacy. As technology accelerates from AI to AGI (2028–2032) to ASI (2032–2036), staying relevant means adapting fast. Legacy isn't about titles or trophies. It's about empowering future generations with tools, knowledge, and the mindset to innovate boldly.

AI isn't here to replace the personal touch of leadership; it's here to amplify it. Today's youth are growing up in a world deeply integrated with AI. Their understanding of this tech goes beyond what many of us can imagine, making mentorship vital.

The question is whether we will embrace this new reality or fall behind. Legacy should be about creating lasting impact, building something bigger than ourselves, and empowering future leaders. If we act boldly and think bigger, AI becomes a tool to reshape leadership and leave a mark that outlasts us.

The future isn't coming; it's already here. Observing isn't enough; it's time to lead with AI. This is our chance to shape a world defined by innovation and wisdom. Let's create a legacy that truly matters.

How I evolved my thinking as both a parent and advocate for AI

> *"We don't inherit the earth from our ancestors; we borrow it from our children."*
> — Native American Proverb

When I first started thinking about *legacy*, it seemed pretty simple. I just wanted to leave something behind that would mean something for my kids—something pow'erful, as my parents did for our 65 godchildren spread across five continents. I wanted them to have the same values I grew up with: work hard, be kind, and make a real difference. But then, as I dug deeper into the world of AI and leadership, it hit me: my whole idea of legacy needed to shift. The world is changing faster than we can keep up with, and the tools we have to shape it are transforming right before our eyes. What, I thought, would be enough?

The future isn't waiting for us to catch up. It's moving forward, and it's time we think bigger. It's time to think bolder and smarter about the legacy we want to leave. As a father, proud Rotarian, and someone deeply invested in the future of the **next generation**, I knew that I had to give my kids something more than just the basics. The world they're stepping into is going to be so different from the one I grew up in. That's when it hit me: AI could be the game changer. This isn't about just passing down advice; it's about giving them the tools, the mindset, and the power to do things bigger than I ever could. It's about preparing them to lead, to create, and to adapt in ways we can't even begin to imagine. The future of leadership isn't about following the path. It's about **creating new paths**. And AI is the key that will help them do that.

Now let me tell you why this is so personal. For me, **AI didn't just help me. It saved my life**. After a near-fatal accident left me with a severe brain injury, I was physically fine, but mentally? I was a shell of myself. My cognitive function was like that of a child. I couldn't think. I couldn't focus. I couldn't process. But here's the crazy part: my dad, a tech pioneer, had me learning AI back in 1996, before most people even knew it existed. He sat me in front of computers day after day, **retraining my brain** with AI. And that became my therapy. It became my tool for recovery. Slowly, piece by piece, I started to recover.

I've always believed that a legacy isn't about what you leave behind; it's about how you empower others. **Maya Angelou once said, "Your legacy is every life you've touched."** That really stuck with me. I realized my legacy wouldn't be about material things or just lessons. It's about inspiring the next generation, giving them the tools to lead in ways we can't even imagine yet, and giving them the power to carry that torch and take leadership to places we've never thought possible. That's how we build something that lasts—not by what we leave behind, but by empowering others to do more than we ever could.

When I was growing up, I was taught the importance of **giving back**, of helping others so they could thrive. But it wasn't until I became a father myself that I truly saw the world differently. Life stopped being just about me. It became about what I could do for my children and the world they would inherit. And right around that time, the world started waking up to the power of Generative AI.

While many are chasing the **next big thing** in AI, I was thinking about something deeper—about the role AI would play in the legacy I'm building for my kids and the generations to come. That question became the heart of everything I'm doing. It's not just about using AI; it's about leading with it. It's about guiding others not just with strategies, but with **heart and vision**. It's about looking beyond the surface, beyond the headlines, and seeing the real potential of AI. This isn't just the next big trend. It's a tool that will help us go far beyond what we ever thought was possible. This is about creating a future where every life we touch is empowered to do incredible things. And that's the kind of legacy I want to build.

AI as a Legacy Builder - How to Build a Future-Proof Leadership

"AI will be remembered in history as either humanity's greatest tool or its final mistake. Our legacy depends on how we wield it."
— *Stephen Hawking*

Leadership isn't about "being the boss" anymore. It's about **creat-**

ing a legacy that empowers people to take action, innovate, and do things that truly matter. And if you're thinking about future-proofing your leadership, you **can't afford to ignore AI.**

Why? Because AI can make you smarter, faster, and more effective as a leader. Whether you're making big decisions or guiding a team, AI can **analyze massive amounts of data** and give you insights that allow you to act with **precision.** But the key to future-proofing leadership is **how you use AI,** not just how much you rely on it.

AI for smarter, faster decisions

In a fast-paced world, quick decision-making is key. AI can process mountains of data in real time, helping leaders spot patterns, trends, and potential risks way faster than any human could. And when you add **emotional intelligence (EQ)** to the mix, it's like **supercharging** your leadership ability.

Think about it. AI gives you the data to make decisions, and EQ gives you the **human touch** to know how to act on it. You get the best of both worlds.

Abraham Lincoln said: **"The best way to predict the future is to create it."** By combining the power of AI and human insight, you're not just predicting the future—you're **shaping it.**

Emotional Intelligence: The secret sauce of leadership

AI is incredible for making data-driven decisions, but it doesn't replace the need for emotional intelligence. AI can't connect with people on a human level. That's where EQ comes in.

When you lead with emotional intelligence, you're not just making decisions based on logic; you're taking into account **how people feel.** You're understanding what motivates them, what challenges they're facing, and what gets them excited. That kind of insight can't be replaced by any algorithm.

Simon Sinek said, **"Leadership is not about being in charge. It's**

about taking care of those in your charge." If you're leading with heart and understanding, people are going to **follow you** because they trust you. And trust is a key part of leaving a **lasting legacy.**

Mentorship and Generational Shift:
How to include younger leaders in today's leadership

"Do something wonderful, people may imitate it."
— *Albert Schweitzer*

One thing that's becoming clear is that the **next generation of leaders** is already here—and they're way ahead of where we were at their age. These young leaders grew up in a world where technology was part of their everyday life. They "get" AI. More importantly, they understand how it can be used to **solve some of the world's biggest problems.** As leaders today, we can't afford to ignore this.

We have to be **intentional about mentoring** the younger generation. But mentorship isn't just about passing down knowledge. It's about creating the space for them to lead in their own way, to find their voice, and to step up in ways we never could. The future is theirs, and it's time we made sure they have everything they need to succeed.

AI and mentorship - a powerful combo

Mentorship has always been about that **personal connection,** the kind of **trust and guidance** that builds leaders. It's about sitting down, sharing knowledge, and empowering someone to take charge of their journey. That's timeless.

But now, AI is flipping the script. It's not here to replace the magic of human mentorship. It's here to amplify it. Think about it: **AI-powered platforms match the right mentors with the right mentees,** no matter where they are in the world. AI helps spark conversations, offers insights, and gives feedback that helps everyone grow, whether they're in the same city or on opposite sides of the globe.

Here's the real win, though: AI doesn't take away the personal touch; it **supercharges** it. Mentorship stays rooted in connection and trust, but AI lets us scale it, making sure every interaction is intentional and impactful. It's not about teaching the next generation the rules, but about giving them the tools and freedom to lead in their own way.

This is mentorship on another level. It's **combining old-school wisdom with cutting-edge tech** to make sure no one gets left behind. That's how you create leaders, and that's how you change the game.

Including young voices in leadership

If we want to future-proof leadership, we've got to make sure we're bringing young voices to the table. This generation is already comfortable with technology, and they're full of fresh, **innovative ideas** on how to use it to change the world. By including them in leadership, we're making sure decisions are shaped by both **experience and new, forward-thinking vision.**

Think about it. According to the Harward Law Corporate Business Forum, the average age of directors of today's most successful US companies, including unicorns and trillion-dollar enterprises, is approximately 63 years. Newer high-growth companies have boards with an average age of 36; with startups and scaleups, ideally, it's even younger—closer to 27.

It's time we started listening to the younger generation. **As John C. Maxwell says, "Mentoring is not about molding a perfect replica of yourself. It's about helping someone else find their own path."**

The generational shift isn't something to be afraid of. It's something we need to embrace if we want to leave behind a legacy that matters, one that will shape the future for years to come. By bringing young leaders in now, we're setting the stage for a better tomorrow. The future is theirs, and we need to give them the platform to lead.

The Sensory Leader - Using AI and Empathy to Lead Wisely

"Our legacy will not be written in books, but in the algorithms that shape the future."
— *Ray Kurzweil, Computer Scientist and Futurist*

Leadership is about **understanding people**—their fears, their dreams, their motivations. As leaders, we have to be able to **feel** the energy of the room, understand what's going on beneath the surface, and **connect with people** in a meaningful way.

Leading with heart and data

You can't ignore the importance of data, but also, you can't overlook the importance of **human connection**. The best leaders combine the analytical power of AI with the **emotional intelligence** to know when to act with compassion, empathy, and understanding. When you lead with both your heart and your mind, you'll inspire those around you in ways that make an **impact**.

As John Wooden once said, "The most powerful leadership tool you have is your own example." If you lead by example, using both the power of AI and the strength of your own emotions, you'll inspire others to do the same.

"AI will either amplify the best of humanity or automate the worst of us—the legacy is ours to define." — *Yuval Noah Harari*

So, what's the secret to building a leadership legacy that stands the test of time?

It's simple: **embrace change, take action, and empower others**.

1. **Leverage AI as a tool:** Don't see AI as a threat—use it to enhance your decision-making, efficiency, and leadership skills.

2. **Develop emotional intelligence:** Know when to rely on data and when to lead with empathy. Your **EQ** is just as important as your IQ.

3. **Mentor the next generation:** Invest in younger leaders, giving them the tools and space to grow and innovate.

4. **Commit to continuous learning:** The future is moving lightning fast. To stay relevant, you need to stay ahead of the curve.

5. **Lead with ethical responsibility:** Use AI responsibly and always keep the **well-being of people** in mind.

By doing these things, you'll not only be building a legacy, you'll be future-proofing it in a way that empowers others to carry the torch and do great things.

Nick

About Nick Sinanan

Nick Sinanan is a multi award-winning author, global speaker and visionary leader. He has been referred to as "Wall Street's Leading Peak Performance Strategist" with 25+ years of expertise in psychological high performance and philanthropy. Honored globally, Nick's mission is to empower one billion people by 2030 through financial independence, leveraging AI and innovation to create lasting global impact.

www.nick-sinanan.com

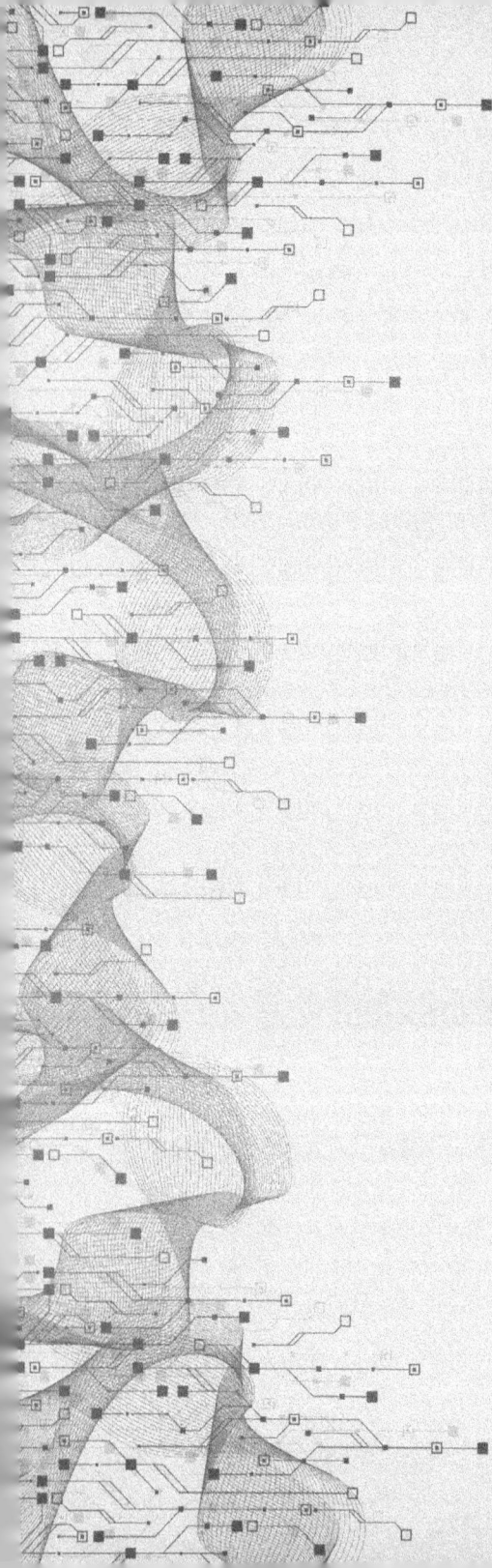

SESSION FOUR

Marketing

David Gomez
Melitta Campbell

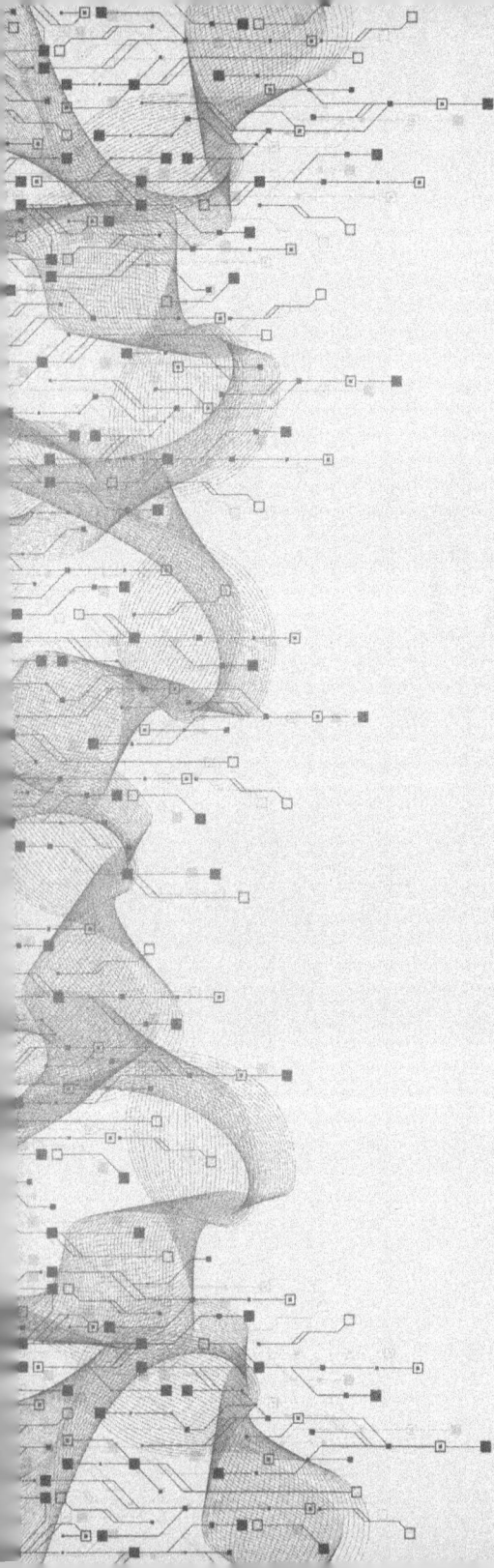

Welcome to the Marketing Session

Welcome to the Marketing session of Connect, Lead, Succeed—where we explore how great businesses don't just exist... they connect, communicate, and convert with purpose.

In this session, we bring together two powerhouse voices in ethical, effective marketing—each offering fresh perspectives on how to build trust, attract the right clients, and grow with intention.

First, we have **David Gomez**, bestselling author and marketing strategist, with his chapter asking the tough questions like: Why should I choose you? David unpacks the critical importance of clear differentiation in a crowded market. His keynote reads like a masterclass in value articulation—helping you position your product, service, or personal brand so precisely that your ideal clients won't just notice you... they'll remember you.

Then, we welcome **Melitta Campbell**, award-winning business coach and mentor for female entrepreneurs. Melitta shows how modern marketing can be both strategic and heart-centered. She brings a refreshing approach that blends storytelling, service, and confidence, helping business owners attract aligned clients without resorting to pushy tactics or hype.

Together, David and Melitta show us that marketing isn't about being loud. It's about being clear, consistent, and connected to what truly matters to your audience.

This is marketing with meaning.

Let's dive in.

Introducing David Gomez

Please welcome to the stage one of the leading voices in value-based selling—David Gomez. With experience in over 450 organizations across 21 countries, David has helped companies defend their value, avoid destructive discounting, and stand out in commoditized markets. He's the best-selling author of Stop Competing on Price, and today, he'll challenge everything you thought you knew about pricing, differentiation, and winning the right clients. Get ready to discover why the best sales strategy isn't lowering your price—it's proving you're worth it.

CHAPTER TWELVE

Stop Competing on Price

*Don't sell yourself short—sell
what makes you different.*

The goal of any business is to make money—or at least be sustainable. And each company chooses its own path: some compete on low prices; others go mid-range, premium, or use a mix of strategies. No strategy is inherently right or wrong. Some are simply more viable than others, depending on a company's competitive position, financial strength, and ability to execute consistently.

---

*Lowering prices to win sales is easy—and risky. The
real challenge is doing it profitably.*

Few things destroy a company's value faster than offering low prices without extreme efficiency, economies of scale, consistent quality, tough vendor negotiations, and a marketing strategy built around price. That's why very few businesses can successfully compete on price alone.

Why the dangerous habit of discounting?

Many companies—and their sales teams—are better trained to negotiate a discount than to argue the benefits that justify their price. Instead of defending their value based on the rewards they bring to clients, they default to lowering the price. After working with sales teams for decades, I've found these to be the most common reasons:

- **Fear of losing the sale** – When commissions and bonuses are tied to hitting a sales quota, salespeople often feel more pressure than the buyer. Without a clear profile of the ideal client, they treat every prospect as a must-win, making discounts their default tool.

- **Weak differentiation** – Vague or generic pitches don't justify premium pricing. Customers need a clear, specific reason to choose you. One sales team I worked with was successfully persuaded to sell higher-priced acupuncture needles by explaining they stayed sharper longer, thus reducing patient discomfort. Doctors could proudly share that benefit with their patients.

- **Poor understanding of competitors** – Knowing what your competitors charge isn't enough. Many buyers know more about your rivals than you do. If you don't know *how* you're different, you can't defend your price.

- **Not understanding client needs** – If you don't deeply understand what your clients value, your pitch will sound like everyone else's—focused on features instead of what really matters to them. This goes beyond the traditional arguments about features vs benefits. It's more about how the targeted customer wants, feels, yearns for, or desires something.

How to Stop Competing on Price

Ironically, many companies that generate significant *value* often still end up competing on price. Their outstanding attributes fail to create enough impact in the market. Time and again, the reasons are the same: they're targeting the wrong customers, they lack true differentiation, or if they *are* different, they're not communicating it clearly enough for customers to recognize and pay for it.

To break free from price-based competition once and for all, you need to do three things:

- Focus on the right clients—those who truly appreciate the value you deliver.
- Be *remarkably* different, so your higher price is easy to justify.
- Communicate that difference clearly, compellingly, and unmistakably, so customers not only understand it but believe it's worth paying for.

1. Focus on the Right Client

To charge a higher price, you first need to narrow your focus. Companies struggle if they try to sell to everyone. Not everyone is your customer, and not everyone deserves your best price.

The wider the net, the weaker the catch. When you try to be everything to everyone, you end up being nothing to anyone.

The key to defending your price begins with choosing who you want to serve. Start by identifying your top 20% of customers, the ones who are profitable, easy to work with, and truly value what you offer. Then focus on finding more clients like them. That's where your energy should go.

Take the example of a client I recently worked with in the commercial furniture industry. By segmenting their customer base, they discovered that only a handful of industries truly valued their ergonomic innovations.

Stop wasting time trying to convince people who don't appreciate what you offer. Instead, focus on delighting those who do.

By tailoring their messaging and sales strategy to those specific segments, they boosted conversions—without lowering prices.

The core idea is this: define the market segments where your product or service is more relevant than the alternatives. Stop wasting time trying to convince people who don't appreciate what you offer. Instead, focus on delighting those who do.

What Makes an Ideal Client... Ideal?

- **They're profitable** – You can't grow *your* business, improve service, expand distribution, or invest in marketing if your clients aren't already profitable.

- **They value your added benefits** – If your clients don't appreciate what they're getting, either you're targeting the wrong audience or your message isn't clear enough.

- **They get real results** – Your solution isn't a perfect fit for everyone. It works *best* for the exact kind of customer it was designed for. Understand and target your customers' wants, needs, fears, and desires.

- **They promote your business** – The right clients become your best advocates. If your solution worked for them, they'll recommend it. But no one will speak well of a product or experience that fell short of expectations.

How to identify your ideal clients

Clients who constantly haggle, undervalue what you do, or have poor payment practices often cost more than they're worth.

Start by looking at your current customer base and ask yourself: *If I had ten more clients just like this one, would my business thrive?* That's the litmus test. Then, identify what makes those clients ideal. Consider factors like industry, size, mindset, challenges, or purchasing behavior.

Equally important is identifying who *isn't* a good fit: clients who constantly haggle, undervalue what you do, or have poor payment practices. These clients often cost more than they're worth.

For example, while working with a leading industrial supplier, we discovered that their most profitable clients weren't the biggest ones. Instead, their best customers were those who appreciated just-in-time delivery and valued the continuous innovations offered in product design and logistics. That insight transformed their entire strategy.

Another great example is the company that discovered that some higher-value contracts actually worked out to be lower value in profitability because it took longer to get paid, and those clients haggled constantly for "deals" that undermined that company's margins and cashflow.

Create detailed client profiles that capture needs, priorities, and values. Then focus your marketing, sales, and service efforts where the match is strongest. Your best clients deserve your best attention.

What they look like

- Your ideal clients aren't just companies or accounts; they're people. People with goals, frustrations, deadlines, and pressure. Don't label them "B2B" or "B2C". See them as human.
- Understand what matters most to them and connect your

differentiator directly to that. They're not the ones who ask, *"Why is it so expensive?"* They're the ones who say, *"How soon can we start?"* because they see the value.

- Exercise: Create a "Client Snapshot" of your five best customers. What do they have in common? What do they care about? What could you say to attract more people like them?

"Wrong customers are lost because of price. The good ones, because of poor service."
— David Gomez

---

2. Be Remarkably Different

Differentiation isn't about claiming you're better. It's about proving it in a way your customers care about.

Think of differentiation as your armor in a price war. When competitors start slashing prices, you protect your margins by offering what others can't or what they don't know how to communicate. Differentiation isn't about claiming you're better. It's about *proving* it in a way your customers care about.

When two or more options look similar, and no clear benefit sets one apart, customers will default to the only metric they can easily compare: price. But the real issue isn't that customers focus too much on price. It's that many businesses fail to communicate their differences in a way that's obvious and compelling. If clients can't *see* your value, they won't *pay* for it.

Ways to differentiate

Ask yourself: *Why is our price higher?* Sit down with your team and list every reason your product or service costs more than the competition's. In many cases, a higher price means better design, more robust support, or added value. If customers are pushing back, those benefits likely aren't being communicated effectively. You need to ensure that your entire team (not just the sales people) understands why you are more expensive and that they believe in the value your company offers.

Better solutions cost more. That's fair. But if there's a price premium without a clear benefit, there's a problem with your value proposition. And if the benefit is clear to you but not to the client, then the problem is in your communication. For example, having a global presence might seem impressive, but unless it directly benefits the local customer, it's irrelevant to them.

Focus on What Matters to the Buyer

Here are a few areas that often make a real difference:

- **Highly professional salespeople** – A great sales experience saves the customer time and delivers better solutions. A well-trained, knowledgeable salesperson can solve problems faster and more effectively.

- **Information systems** – What seems like an internal advantage can impact clients directly. Robust systems improve inventory control, order tracking, and on-time deliveries—things your customers care about.

- **Being there when it counts** – When things are running smoothly, every supplier looks good. But when problems arise, reliability becomes priceless. Make sure clients know you're the partner who shows up when it matters most.

- **Technical support** – Especially in industrial markets, expert support can be the difference between average results and breakthrough performance. Trained professionals with access to the latest tools and AI can dramatically boost productivity.

- **Certifications** – An ISO certification isn't just a badge; it's proof of standardization and reliability. It tells your client there's no improvisation—only tested, repeatable processes that bring peace of mind. Don't just display the certification; explain what it means to them.

- **Proven experience** – Experience isn't about time served; it's about having overcome challenges. If you've already solved the problems your clients are facing, you're a safer bet than a less seasoned competitor.

- **Integrated supply chain** – The ability to deliver the right product, at the right time, in the right quantity, is a game changer. It directly impacts your client's profitability, and it's a key advantage when competing with overseas suppliers.

- Customization – Tailoring your offer to the client's specific needs can set you apart. Whether it's faster turnaround, fewer intermediaries, or special requirements, flexibility creates value.

"Don't try to be better at everything. Be dramatically better at one thing your customer truly cares about."
— David Gomez

How to create a strong differentiator

Ask your best clients:

- Why did you choose us?
- What surprised you?
- What would you miss if we were gone?

These insights are gold. They reveal what truly matters to your clients and are often things you've overlooked or undervalued.

I once encouraged a regional bank to ask their clients these questions. The most common response wasn't about interest rates or digital tools. It was, *"You actually pick up the phone and know our names."* That small detail became the heart of their marketing message. It wasn't flashy, but it was powerful.

In another case, a dentist discovered that her edge wasn't the latest technology but the way she helped patients manage anxiety. That insight shifted her brand positioning and completely transformed her patients' waiting room experience.

A powerful differentiator should be:

- Unique in the eyes of your market – if a competitor can claim it, it's not yours.
- Valued by your ideal customer – if your client doesn't care, it's irrelevant.
- Easy to explain and demonstrate – if you can't prove it, it won't sell.

EXCERCISE:

Use this three-filter test on each of your current selling points. Which ones fail? Which ones can be reframed or expanded? Which ones could become your signature difference?

"Be different or be gone." — *David Gomez*

3. Express Your Uniqueness Clearly

Businesses don't lose sales for a lack of value. They lose them for a lack of clarity.

Businesses don't lose sales for a lack of value. They lose them for a lack of clarity.

We live in a noisy marketplace. If your message doesn't cut through, it gets ignored. Jargon, buzzwords, and vague claims like "great service" or "high quality" don't help. *They make you blend in, not stand out.*

Clarity beats cleverness. Precision beats fluff. If your client doesn't instantly get what makes you different and why it matters to them, you've lost the sale before it begins.

Instead of saying, *"We offer excellent service,"* say, *"We respond to every enquiry within 30 minutes."* That's clear. It's credible. And it's easy to remember.

Crafting effective communication

To make your message stick, use tools that create contrast, connection, and confidence:

- **Numbers** – *"97% customer retention rate"* is more convincing than *"Most of our customers are loyal."*

- **Client stories** – Real examples create real belief.

- **Contrast** – Don't just show what you do. Show what's at stake if they don't choose you.

- **Humor** – If your tone allows, humor humanizes and connects.

- **Visuals** – A picture or diagram can make your message click instantly.

- **Headlines** – Make every word earn its place. Lead with what matters.

Exercise:

Pick your main sales channel (email, social media, proposals, website—whatever drives your business). Review the last five pieces of communication you sent. Did they say something specific? Did they highlight something different? Did they show something valuable? If not, rewrite them.

"The best communication is the one people understand." — David Gomez

---

Three Things You Can Do Right Now

If you want to stop competing on price, here are three actions you can take immediately:

1. **Revisit your ideal customer**. Look at your 80/20. Who are the top 20% of clients who bring 80% of your value? Refine their profile. Double down on finding more like them.

2. **Define your real differentiator**. Gather your team and ask: *"What do we do that others don't?"* And *"Does the customer actually care?"* Choose one thing—and own it.

3. **Improve how you communicate it**. Test your message. Ask: Could a 12-year-old understand it? Could your client repeat it to their boss? If not, rewrite it. Clear wins over clever, every time.

Final reflection

You don't need lower prices. You need better arguments.

You don't need more clients. You need the right ones.

You don't need to scream louder. You need to say something worth hearing.

Stop competing on price. Start defending your value.

Want to go deeper?

Explore the ideas in this chapter further in my books *Stop Competing on Price* and *It's the Small Things*. They're both filled with stories, tools, and frameworks to help you build a business that people are happy to pay more for.

Let's make your value visible.

David

About David Gomez

When organizations want to increase profitability, stop competing on price, and clearly demonstrate their value to customers, they call David Gomez.

David is a renowned international speaker and bestselling author of seven books in Spanish, several of which have been translated into English. His masterpiece, *Stop Competing on Price*—widely known as the bible of value selling—is a required reference in business programs at multiple universities in Latin America and is implemented by hundreds of companies around the world.

Another of his bestsellers, *It's the Small Things*, has become the go-to practical guide for organizations seeking to stand out by creating memorable customer experiences in a simple yet powerful way.

David has helped over 450 organizations across 21 countries and five continents defend their value, highlight their differentiators, and negotiate without lowering their prices. His proprietary methodology—proven over the years across dozens of industries—transforms brands in commoditized markets into value leaders, driving stronger customer loyalty and sustained profitability.

Want more practical tools? Download my free resource, *50 Differentiation Arguments*, a guide to help you build and express what makes your business worth paying more for.

https://davidgomez.co/wp-content/uploads/50-Differentiation-Arguments.pdf

www.davidgomez.co

Introducing Melitta Campbell, Switzerland

Please welcome Melitta Campbell — a TEDx speaker, bestselling author, and multi-award-winning business coach known as The Value Whisperer. With experience at Nestlé, Lloyds Bank, and the UN, Melitta has helped hundreds of entrepreneurs and leaders communicate their value with clarity and confidence. Her signature Value Whispering methodology empowers business owners to stop chasing attention and start resonating deeply with the right people. Through her engaging talks and podcast, The Art of Value Whispering, Melitta delivers a powerful three-step framework that helps even the most introverted entrepreneur to thrive without compromising who they are. Get ready to be inspired, uplifted, and equipped for impact!

CHAPTER THIRTEEN

Marketing Your True Value with a Whisper

Two months after the birth of my first daughter, it became clear that returning to the corporate career I loved was not going to be possible. Not wanting to withdraw from my career completely, I started a communication consultancy during my baby's nap times, and within a year I was advising communication teams and leaders within some of the world's largest organizations, such as Lloyds Bank, Nestlé, and the UN.

It was exciting at first, and I loved the chance to be the kind of mum I wanted to be while still getting to use my marketing and communication skills to earn an income. Eight years on, I looked like a big success. But on the inside, I was struggling and found myself facing burnout. I had forgotten to ask myself an all-important question:

Why? I was attracting well-paid contracts, but it wasn't work that gave me joy, meaning, and energy. Every day became a chore.

Then I read one quote that changed everything! Sir Richard Branson said: "If it's no longer fun, stop doing it." It instantly hit home. Heeding his advice, I looked for a different way to use my skills and experiences to help others.

Then something started happening that led me to the perfect problem to solve.

While networking, I would talk about my work helping corporate leaders to engage their teams. I'd explain how I helped my clients to communicate complex change projects in a straightforward, human-centric way. But then people would respond by asking me to help them grow their small business. I was confused. I was a marketing and communication expert. I wasn't an expert in small business strategy. Why did they think I could help them build their business? I told them no.

That was until I met Ana. She was the sixth person in a row to ask me this question, and she got quite terse on hearing my reply. "But you have to help," she exclaimed. "You're the only one who can!"

I asked what she was seeing in my skillset that I was not. Ana told me about her business and how passionate she was about guiding her coaching clients to results that were well beyond what they expected. The problem was, she wasn't attracting enough of the *right* clients to create a sustainable business. And even when she *did* get in front of an ideal prospect, they just didn't understand her offer in a way that made them want to work with her—at least, not without some serious cajoling and discounting. She was exhausted and disappointed. Marketing her business and attracting clients felt like an impossible challenge. And the effort of trying was causing her to work long hours and miss out on time with her family. She felt as though she was missing a piece of the marketing puzzle, but she just couldn't figure out what that was.

Then she looked me in the eye and quietly said: "You help people communicate in a way that helps others understand and buy into their ideas. I get the sense that that is the missing piece I'm searching for. Will you help me?"

She was right. That was exactly what I did. But I was so close to the work I was doing with corporates, I hadn't seen how my experience could help small business owners too.

That night, I replayed our conversation in my mind. I started to see how I could help small business owners like Ana. As I did, I realized that she was only partially right. It wasn't the ideas or her offer that she needed to communicate, but the *value* of those. That was the missing piece.

Experience had taught me that having great skills, and believing in your ability to use those skills, are two different things.

My mind started racing. I was inspired and excited. At 4:00 a.m., I gave up even trying to get some sleep. Instead, I got up, made a big mug of coffee, fired up my MacBook, and started mapping out my thoughts.

If I was going to help, I knew I needed to cover more than just how to communicate value and market a business. Not that these weren't big enough topics or common enough struggles. But experience had taught me that having great skills, and believing in your ability to use those skills, were two different things. For my work to have an impact, my clients would first need to understand their value *and* believe in it.

I also knew that, like me, many business owners had started their business to secure greater flexibility. They needed a way to work around their family, studies, or other commitments. That meant that time was going to be an issue. And since my clients were likely to be not just time-poor but have fragmented focus too, I'd need to help them find a way to get things done and feel accomplished despite distractions.

Few people are ever taught how to communicate effectively, let alone how to communicate, market, and sell their own brilliance. I would need to fill this gap by helping my clients quickly grasp the essentials of communication, marketing, and sales best practice. This would ensure they didn't just come away from our collaboration with a one-off message to share, but an understanding of how to create meaning, connection, and results through their promotional efforts. This would not only attract more of the right clients and feel natural to do, but, with their existing resources, could grow their business faster.

From this focus, I developed the three core stages of my Value Whispering Blueprint".

1. Identifying your true value (clarifying your values and vision, and creating the right offers for the right clients)
2. Value weaving (mastering meaningful marketing and sales, supported by simple processes)
3. Self-leadership (building your success mindset, habits, and productivity)

To test my Blueprint, I worked with three business owners, each at a different stage of business and all struggling to communicate their value and attract the right clients. As I began to coach them through the three stages, I was convinced my Blueprint would work—but I had no idea how fast. Within weeks, each of my clients felt confident communicating their value in any situation, and they were attracting perfect clients as a result. It was the confirmation I needed to close my communication consultancy and go all in with my Value Whispering Blueprint.

Over the past decade, I've I have seen time after time just how quickly any small business can grow once you understand and take action in these three areas.

Step 1: Understanding Your True Value

It's impossible to embrace and share your value if you don't know what that is. So, this first stage requires some deep reflection to explore the value you can bring to your clients. In their excitement to start their new business, many people miss this stage, and it's why they struggle with their marketing and messaging.

You see, much of your value is buried deep within your life experiences—the changes you've lived through, the lessons you've learned the hard way, and those moments of intense pressure that taught you what you are really capable of. Your *true* value is so much more than just your education and values. It comes from the hard-won insights you've gained over your lifetime. **To start identifying your value, list your strengths, values, and education**. Even if you have already done some work on this, dust it off and refresh it. This information will provide you with an appreciation of your existing toolkit. But don't stop there.

This step can be challenging because all too often, in one way or another, we've learned that talking about our strengths and brilliance is a bad thing. It's bragging. Sharing our failures and flaws is also bad. It shows weakness and suggests we are not good enough. But that leaves us in the middle, feeling ordinary. This is not a place from which we can make a meaningful impact.

So, embrace it all. You'll soon see that you've been gifted a one-of-a-kind perspective and vision that no one else has. This is your true value.

When you add to this a deeper understanding of your dream client—their challenges, values, and aspirations—you can start to see just how you can use your value to help them live their ideal life. I call this overlap your Value Sweet Spot. Once you know that, you'll be ready for step two: Value Weaving.

Sarah's story: When I started working with Sarah, she was disappointed with her sales results. In her conversations, when she explained all the different ways she could help, few of her prospects bought into her services, at least not without some serious discounting that eroded her profits. Once she discovered her Value Sweet Spot, Sarah quickly saw how to communicate the value she offered. From her very next sales conversation, her results improved. More clients started saying yes to working with her, since they now understood and appreciated her value. Not only that, but she also stopped discounting, and within weeks she was selling higher-ticket services that enabled her and her team to serve her clients on a deeper level than ever before.

Once you understand and can communicate your true value, you will attract more of the right clients without having to be loud or pushy. You will serve your clients in a deeper and more meaningful way, too.

Step 2: Value Weaving

When you embrace your true value and weave your unique brilliance and perspective into everything you do, all your thoughts, words, and actions will have more meaning and impact. And when you are being yourself, your whisper will create a resonance that attracts the right people and opportunities into your business, allowing you to naturally stand out and create a positive impact through your marketing and sales.

One of the most effective and straightforward ways to weave your value through your messaging and marketing is by using the buyer's journey. This is the series of predictable steps your future clients go through as they discover your solution, determine if it aligns with their needs, values, and aspirations, and assess if they trust you to deliver what you promise.

By creating a series of intentional touchpoints, you can provide the right insight, information, and experience they need to determine if you are the right service provider for them. If you have done the first part of the Value Whispering process well, then creating messages and marketing that resonates with your dream client will be much easier.

Once you have woven your value through your marketing to guide your dream client gently and naturally towards your business, the final stage of the Value Whispering Blueprint ensures you can implement the first step of your plan, and every step that follows, with joy and confidence. It's all about Self-leadership.

Kate's story: For two years, Kate's language school had been losing money. As we explored her true value, we discovered that her niche and message didn't match her value or vision. Once she understood her Value Sweet Spot, Kate instantly changed the way she spoke about her work and adopted a new marketing strategy that felt more aligned and therefore easier and more enjoyable to deliver. Within two months, Kate was consistently enrolling her dream clients and breaking even for the first time. Within six months, she was profitable and had a wait list for her services.

When you understand your true value, weaving this value through your messaging and marketing feels straightforward and natural. And, as your words and actions are closely aligned to your value and vision, you rapidly build "know, like, and trust" with your dream clients, quickly resulting in more impact and profitable business growth.

Step 3: Self-leadership

Through my work over the years, I have noticed that understanding your value and weaving it through your work isn't always enough. Self-doubt can creep in, and conflicting demands can throw you off track. This can weaken your whisper, leaving you with an indistinct murmur. To avoid this, the final step requires you to build your self-belief, habits, and boundaries.

> *Look back to those moments when you have made yourself proud, and at the praise you've received from others. Explore what this information tells you about your ability to make a difference, and the conditions you need to make things happen.*

Start by looking back to those moments when you made yourself proud, and at the praise you received from others. Explore what this information tells you about your ability to make a difference and the conditions you need to make things happen. Then boldly create the environment and a set of priorities that support your success and protect your ability to show up as your best self. Put boundaries around these to protect your time, energy, and focus. And then stick to those boundaries as if your business and your ability to make a difference depend on them—because they do!

I also suggest creating a Success Journal to accompany your business growth. Each day, write two or three things you have achieved that you feel proud of. These needn't be big things, but anything you completed or realized and felt good about. Then show yourself gratitude by also noting down your appreciation of your skills and tenacity in making these positive steps happen. Review your journal regularly to help you consistently build your confidence and momentum.

Paulina's story: Paulina is a talented writer and had adopted a clas-

sic freelance model for her business. But this meant that she was always responding to her client's last-minute demands and had little time to spend with her young daughter. Once Pauliina understood her Value Sweet Spot and her desired lifestyle, she was able to develop a new business model that allowed her to increase the value she offered to her clients, while also creating more time for herself. As she could now also communicate her value clearly, her existing clients were happy to move to her new way of working and even pay higher fees. This move gave her more time and control with which to launch an online program to diversify her income and take her first family holiday for three years.

Having a business that gives you the freedom you desire happens not by accident but by design. Once you understand how you can best create value, you can focus and deliver this in ways that support your preferred lifestyle. Cultivating your working environment, mindset, and boundaries will be the key to lasting satisfaction and a growing business.

Allowing your diamond to shine

When I think about the Value Whispering Blueprint, it feels like mining for that diamond within.

First, you dig deep to find that seam, rich in potential value.

Then, you chip away at the rock to reveal the precious stone inside.

Then, you give the gem a shape suitable for its final purpose.

Finally, you polish it and proudly share it with the world. And when you do, and the light finds your diamond and refracts, dozens of small beams of light go off in all directions, each one creating a captivating rainbow on any surface it touches.

When you whisper your value through everything you do, your

"diamond within" creates this wonderful kaleidoscope effect that has a positive impact in often unexpected ways, but always with beautiful results.

That's what I love most about Value Whispering. Over the last eight years, I have guided hundreds of business owners through the Value Whispering Blueprint. And still, with each new client, new member of my community, or new listener of my podcast, I can never quite predict just how far the concept will take them. Because once they tap into their true value, believe in their abilities, and start to take action, they start to dream bigger and achieve more than they previously imagined.

As you start sharing your value, I want you to remember one thing: success isn't about shouting the loudest; it's about resonating the deepest. Do this and you won't need to shout, because your whisper is already loud enough.

Melitta

About Melitta Campbell

Melitta Campbell, *The Value Whisperer*, is an award-winning business coach, TEDx speaker, podcast host and bestselling author. With a background in marketing and communication that spans three decades, she helps entrepreneurs and leaders confidently express their true value and quietly grow their influence. Drawing on her experience with global organizations like Nestlé and the UN, Melitta developed the Value Whispering methodology—a powerful approach to meaningful communication and business growth that allows business owners and leaders to create impact without compromising who they are.

www.melittacampbell.com

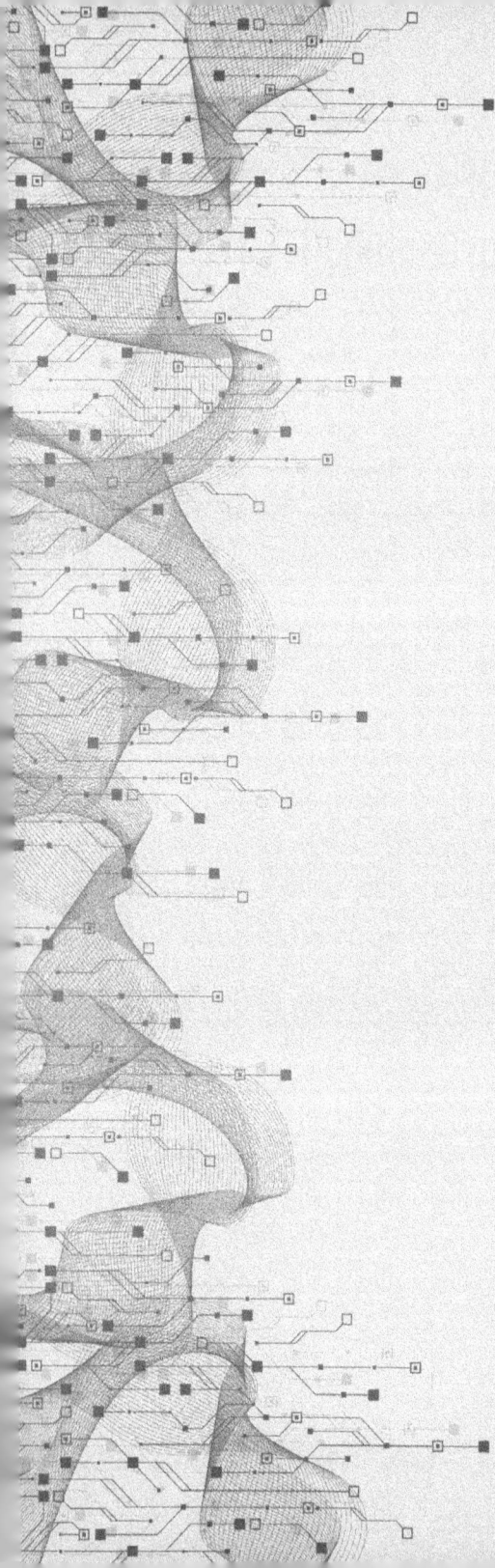

Networking

Pavel Verbnyak

Yabeejan Koya

Julie Nottage

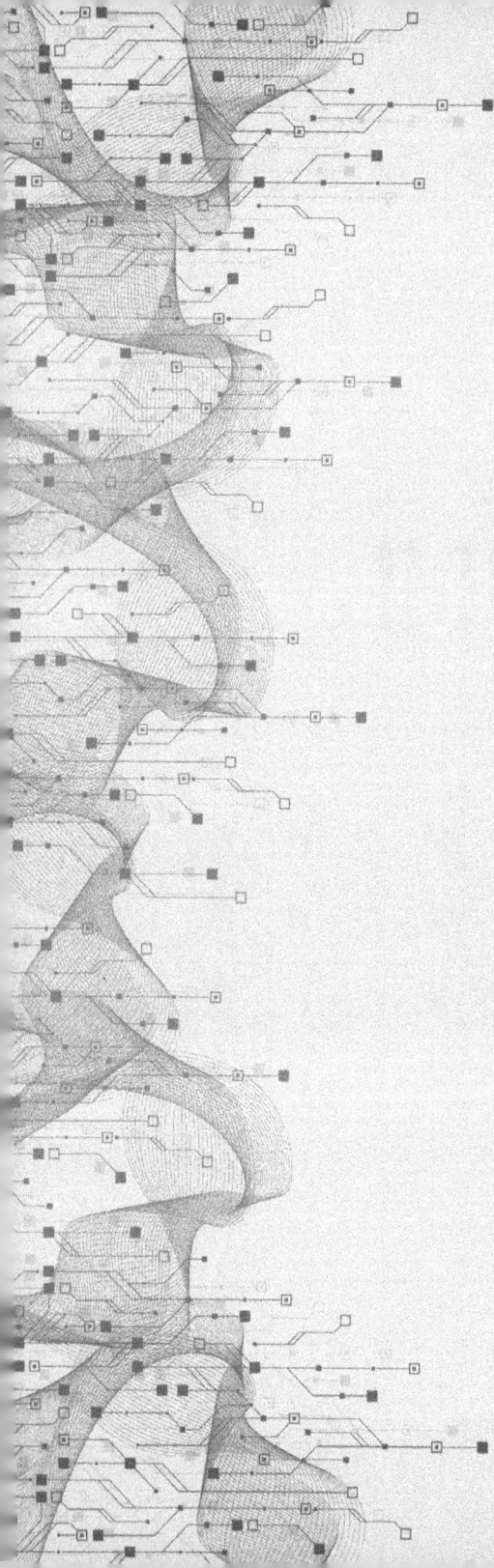

Welcome to the Networking Session

Alright, conference attendees, put down the business cards and step away from the awkward small talk. This isn't your average networking session. This is where we take the tired "who do you know?" cliché and flip it into something far more powerful: **Who knows you, and why should they care?**

Welcome to the Connect, Lead, Succeed Networking Session, where we get strategic, soulful, and just a little cheeky about building real connections that actually matter.

First up, **Pavel Verbnyak** *reveals how networking and connecting at a global level requires strategy, personal energy, and emotional intelligence because the most successful people don't collect contacts, they cultivate champions.*

Next, **Yabeejan Koya** *shakes things up with focusing on making all your networking a human connection experience, not just a business exercise. A passionate leadership developer and team building expert, Yabeejan pulls no punches about what real connection looks like in today's world. It's not about being everywhere—it's about showing up with purpose and presence where it counts.*

And finally, **Julie Nottage** *wraps this session with her delightfully unconventional take on Confidence is your Catalyst for Business Growth. Julie invites us to break the traditional rules of networking and leads instead with curiosity, generosity, and a bit of joyful mischief.*

So if you thought networking was a dry LinkedIn exercise—think again. Let's make it matter.

Let's get connected.

Introducing Pavel Verbnyak, Russia

Imagine being able to walk into any room—whether in Moscow, Mumbai, or Manhattan—and leave with meaningful connections that open doors. Our next speaker has mastered this art. From humble beginnings in Russia to coaching Fortune 500 leaders, Pavel Verbnyak reveals how human connection fuels success. His chapter, International Networking, distills decades of global experience into three principles anyone can use—proving that opportunity isn't about who you know, but how you know them.

Please welcome a man who's as generous as he is insightful, Pavel Verbnyak!

CHAPTER FOURTEEN

International Networking

I grew up in Petrozavodsk, a small town surrounded by forests and lakes in north-west Russia. From a young age, I was immersed in the world of biathlon. The sport shaped my character and taught me that, even in individual competitions, victory is always a team effort. Coaches, teammates, family, and mentors all play their part. Without their support, no success is truly sustainable.

Perhaps the most powerful influence on my ability to connect with people came from someone very close to me—my grandfather. A World War II veteran and a respected figure in our town, he had an extraordinary gift. *He genuinely loved people.* He didn't seek personal gain from his conversations; he simply listened, offered wisdom, and gave warmth. Observing him as a boy, I wondered why some people effortlessly create strong connections, while others struggle for years.

That curiosity sparked a journey. I began to study biographies of influential people from various fields. Over time, a common thread emerged: they had all developed the skill of intentional networking.

Later, I had the privilege of studying in the United States under Jack Canfield, one of the great teachers of personal development. I realized something crucial: networking isn't a matter of luck or charm. It's a skill. A learnable, repeatable, improvable skill. One that can open doors you didn't even know existed.

Since that time, I've dedicated my life to mastering this skill and sharing it with others. From moving to Moscow and launching my coaching and training business to working alongside global thought leaders and delivering seminars around the world, my path has shown me one truth over and over again:

> *The ability to build meaningful connections is one of the greatest assets you can develop.*

I've been privileged to coach top executives, host leadership retreats, speak at international forums, and train thousands of people, from students to CEOs. I've run a marathon, authored several books, and interviewed over 500 remarkable individuals across business, science, arts, and sports. And yes, my journey also included washing dishes in the US back in 2008, when I first learned how humble beginnings can become powerful stepping stones.

> *Human connection is the golden thread woven through every opportunity, every leap, every breakthrough.*

But no matter where I went or what I achieved, the essence of success remained the same: people. Human connection is the golden thread woven through every opportunity, every leap, every breakthrough.

The three principles of networking that work anywhere in the world

1. Give before you ask

Many years ago, I met the owner of a large international business. Instead of jumping into a pitch or asking for a favor, I simply asked him what he was passionate about outside of work. He lit up and began telling me about his love for skiing. As an athlete myself, I had plenty to share, and the conversation flowed naturally. He later offered me a collaboration without my needing to ask.

Lesson: Don't lead with "What can I get?" Lead with "How can I help?" Even small acts—an introduction, a thoughtful article, a sincere compliment—build trust and goodwill.

The world remembers givers. Giving doesn't mean overextending yourself. It means showing genuine interest and generosity in your energy, attention, and resources.

2. Listen like they're the only person in the room

In Malaysia, I once met an investor who spent nearly an hour sharing his journey. I didn't interrupt or steer the conversation. I just listened, asked questions, and held space. At the end, he said, "You're the first person who's actually listened to me in years."

In a world that's obsessed with speaking, **listening is a superpower.**

Ask open-ended questions like:

- "How did you come up with that idea?"
- "What inspired you to pursue that path?"
- "What's been the most rewarding part of your work?"

And then—listen. Really listen. With your eyes, your posture, your attention.

Maya Angelou is often quoted as saying, "I've learned that people will forget what you said, people will forget what you did, but people will never forget how you made them feel." She was right. When someone feels seen, heard, and valued in your presence, they'll never forget you.

3. Nurture your relationships

Networking is not an event. It's a garden.

One of the biggest mistakes people make is only reaching out when they need something. That's like planting a tree and watering it only when you want fruit.

I have a personal habit that I encourage everyone to adopt:

- Every two to three months, send a quick message to someone in your network just to say hello.
- Share an article, video, or thought that reminded you of them.
- Congratulate them on milestones—not just birthdays, but career wins or personal achievements.

Over time, these small gestures create invisible threads of loyalty, trust, and mutual respect.

Networking Is a Trainable Skill

You don't need to be naturally outgoing to be great at networking. Introverts can be masterful connectors because they tend to listen deeply and create meaningful interactions.

Every skill improves with conscious practice, and networking is no exception. Here's how you can build it like a muscle:

1. **Set a "connection goal."** Challenge yourself to speak to at least one new person at every event.
2. **Use the 3-minute rule:** If you haven't started a conversation

within the first three minutes, approach the nearest person with a smile and introduce yourself.

3. **Keep a networking journal:** Track whom you've helped, followed up with, and stayed in touch with. Over time, you'll see how much impact you're creating.

When I started my journey, I wasn't a polished speaker or a seasoned trainer. I just had curiosity and a genuine desire to grow. Through thousands of interactions, I developed the confidence, presence, and empathy that now shape my coaching and seminars.

My journey with the experts

I've had the honor of working with and learning from some of the greatest minds in personal development. As well as studying under Jack Canfield (as mentioned earlier), I was part of teams trained by Tony Robbins and Joe Dispenza. I've shared stages with incredible thought leaders. But each of them emphasized the same foundational truth:

Success begins with connection—connection with others, and connection with your true self.

These mentors didn't just teach tactics. They lived the principles. They served first. They listened deeply. They nurtured their networks. And now, I do the same.

Through my coaching programs and live workshops, I help individuals and companies build authentic relationships, expand their influence, and lead from a place of service. Whether in boardrooms or classrooms, on cruise ships or university campuses, I've seen the same principles work again and again.

Timeless wisdom in human words

Throughout history, the greatest thinkers have left us clues about the power of relationships:

- Some taught that **the richest man is the one with the most friends.**
- Others said that **every person we meet is both a teacher and a mirror.**
- And still others reminded us that **the strength of our network determines the depth of our impact.**

Greatness is never achieved in isolation. The human heart longs for connection, for resonance, for meaningful exchange. When we ignore this truth, we grow lonely, even in crowds. But when we honor it, we build a life of depth, warmth, and opportunity.

The gentle art of friendship

Networking is not manipulation. It is not transactional. It is **the gentle art of making friends.**

It's writing a note to someone who has lost a loved one. It's remembering the name of your barista. It's asking your colleague how their daughter's recital went. It's showing up, consistently and sincerely.

My grandfather once shared an old proverb with me: "If you know how to be a friend, you will never be poor." I carry that with me wherever I go. And I offer it to you.

When the World Is in Flux

In recent years, our view of networking has been put to the test. A global pandemic shut down borders and boardrooms. Conflicts reshaped industries and disrupted supply chains. Economies wobbled. Conferences went virtual. Face-to-face meetings became Zoom windows. Many professionals began to ask: *Can we still build real, lasting relationships in a world that feels so unpredictable?*

The answer is a resounding yes—but it requires adaptability, intentionality, and emotional intelligence.

I remember speaking with a CEO in the early months of 2020.

His international logistics firm had been grounded—literally. Flights were cancelled, partner factories had closed, and his clients were nervous. He admitted something that stuck with me:

"We had invested years into shaking hands. Now we had to build trust through screens."

And that's what they did. They held weekly virtual coffee chats with clients. They checked in with partners without pitching anything. They sent handwritten notes—yes, real ones—across oceans. Not because it was strategic, but because it was sincere. And it worked. When operations resumed, their partners remembered how they had shown up when others went silent.

This is the heart of relationship capital: showing up when it's hard, not just when it's easy.

In uncertain times, people crave certainty—not in outcomes, but in relationships. They look for consistency, empathy, and clarity. They remember who stood by them, listened, and offered value without conditions.

That's networking in the 21st century. It's no longer about quantity; it's about quality. Not about collecting business cards but cultivating trust.

Digital Doesn't Mean Distant

Yes, the tools have changed. But the essence hasn't.

> *The digital space gives us new tools—but it still requires old-school principles.*

In many ways, online platforms have *democratized* networking. A junior analyst in Lagos can connect with a thought leader in London. A startup founder in Jakarta can pitch to investors in New York. A coach in Petrozavodsk can run masterminds with leaders from

Singapore, Dubai, and Cape Town (I've done that myself).

The digital space gives us new tools, but it still requires old-school principles:

- **Show up consistently**: Comment on people's content. Send follow-ups after webinars. Congratulate someone on their post, not just silently like it.

- **Be specific and thoughtful**: "I loved your recent article on sustainable design. It challenged how I approach product development. Would love to hear more about how you see the future of materials in construction."

- **Respect the relationship pace**: Not every contact becomes a friend overnight. But every touchpoint matters. Just like in real life, trust is built in layers.

Remember: even online, people can feel your energy. They can sense if you're genuine. And they'll gravitate toward those who communicate with warmth, curiosity, and integrity.

Case study: Strategic networking in crisis

Let me share a story about a client I recently worked with in Eastern Europe. Let's call her Elina.

Elina led business development for a mid-sized manufacturing firm. When war broke out in a neighboring country, several of her supply lines were severed. Clients were hesitant. The market was frozen in fear.

Instead of going silent, Elina doubled down on *strategic relationship-building*. But not in the usual way. She did three things:

1. **Initiated virtual roundtables**: Once a month, she hosted informal, invite-only Zoom calls with select clients and partners across her network. No pitches. Just open conversations about

navigating uncertainty, shifting trends, and sharing insights. She called them Clarity Circles.

2. **Reached out to competitors**: Yes—competitors. She opened collaborative dialogues with companies in similar sectors to explore joint logistics and procurement. It built trust and even led to a co-production deal.

3. **Became a connector**: She introduced people within her network who needed each other, even when it had no immediate benefit for her. One of those introductions eventually led to a new investor for her firm.

Within 18 months, not only had she stabilized her company's revenue stream, but also her personal reputation had soared. She was now seen as someone who didn't panic. She connected.

The lesson? Leadership isn't just about knowing the answers. It's about creating spaces for connection, clarity, and collaboration—especially when others are pulling away.

The mindset shift – from "networking" to "relationship design"

For many business leaders, the word "networking" still carries a transactional connotation. But the real opportunity lies in a different mindset:

- **It's not about collecting**. It's about curating.
- **It's not about impressing**. It's about *expressing*—your values, your vision, your care.
- **It's not about everyone liking you**. It's about the *right people* trusting you.

Think of it as relationship *design*. Just like you would design a product, a campaign, or a business strategy, design your ecosystem of connections.

Ask yourself:

- Who inspires me and stretches my thinking?
- Who do I admire for their integrity, not just their results?
- Who do I support consistently?
- Where are the gaps in my network—culturally, professionally, or geographically?

Once you know the answers, you can start reaching out with intention.

Micro-Habits to Strengthen Global Connections

Whether you're an executive, entrepreneur, or early-career professional, here are some practical ways to grow your network even when the world feels uncertain:

1. **"Three-minute gratitude"**: Once a week, message someone who made an impact on you recently, or long ago. Tell them why. Don't overthink it. Just send it.

2. **Time-zone networking**: Once a month, wake up early or stay up late to join an event in another time zone. Broaden your circles beyond your continent.

3. **Create cross-border content**: Write a short LinkedIn post reflecting on something you learned from someone in another country or culture. Tag them. Invite discussion.

4. **Ask better questions**: Instead of "What do you do?", ask "What's been lighting you up lately?" or "What's the most surprising thing about your industry right now?"

5. **Be a lighthouse, not a lifeboat**: You don't need to save people—but you *can* be a beacon. Shine steadily. Offer direction. Stay anchored.

Connection is a currency that never devalues

Whether the world is stable or shaking, the power of relationships remains unchanged. In fact, in uncertain times, it becomes even more valuable.

And here's the beautiful paradox: the people who build the best networks aren't usually trying to "network." They're trying to *understand*. To serve. To grow. To love.

So, wherever you are—whether leading a company, building a dream, or finding your way through a season of change—remember:

The next opportunity is not a click away. It's a *connection* away.

Whether you're starting out, rebuilding, or reaching new heights, remember: the next door opens through a conversation. One message. One question. One act of kindness.

In our world, your ability to connect from the heart may become your greatest advantage.

Every relationship you build is a seed. Some will sprout quickly; others will take years. But if you keep watering with kindness, presence, and sincerity, one day you'll look up and find yourself surrounded by a beautiful, abundant network that lifts you higher.

Keep showing up.

Start today.

With warmth and encouragement,

Pavel

"The quality of your life is determined by the quality of your relationships. And every relationship begins with a moment of genuine connection."
— Pavel Verbnyak

About Pavel Verbnyak

Pavel Verbnyak is an international speaker, life and success strategist, and author, who has trained thousands in the art of soft skills and personal development. A former cross-country skier and biathlete turned coach, he blends lessons from sports, global business, and his mentors like Jack Canfield, Brian Tracy, and Tony Robbins.

Let's Connect.

https://www.linkedin.com/in/pavelverbnyak/

Introducing Yabeejan Koya, India

Ladies and gentlemen, it is my honour to introduce **Yabeejan Koya**. He is a seasoned Business and Leadership Coach, Connection Catalyst, and Professional Speaker with over a decade of experience empowering business leaders, entrepreneurs, and organisations. As the Founder Partner of Infinito Business Services, he has impacted over 10,000 individuals through transformative coaching and training. A respected leader in BNI, JCI, Toastmasters, and PSAI, Yabeejan is known for his calm presence, deep insights, and people-first approach. He is also passionate about helping others to unlock growth, influence and opportunities through genuine connections. Please join me in welcoming **Yabeejan** to the stage!

CHAPTER FIFTEEN

Business Networking - The Human-Centric Way

Rethinking networking in a fast-paced world

Business networking often brings to mind images of crowded rooms, forced small talk, and the ritualistic exchange of business cards. We're told that networking is essential for growth, but too often, it feels transactional, superficial, or even exhausting. In a digital-first world overflowing with LinkedIn invites and virtual coffee chats, many professionals still ask: "Why aren't my connections turning into opportunities?"

Here's the truth: traditional networking misses something vital—the human being at the center.

I'd like to invite you to explore a different path: Human-Centric Networking. Forget about collecting contacts or selling yourself.

Switch your focus onto creating authentic, mutual, and lasting relationships. It's about connection with intention—where people feel seen, valued, and inspired to help one another grow.

From elevator pitches to human conversations

I used to think networking was about saying the right thing at the right time, like a perfectly polished elevator pitch. But over time, I realized the most impactful conversations were not the ones I rehearsed. They were the ones where I paused, listened deeply, and allowed space for a real exchange.

I started treating my interactions the way I treat my health—by paying attention. To how I show up. How present I am. How curious I feel. I began practicing mindfulness in my conversations: listening without interrupting, noticing without judging, and seeing the human behind every title.

This shift was subtle, but powerful. When I stopped networking for gain and started connecting to understand, everything changed.

The Core Principles of Human-Centric Networking

Human-centric networking goes well beyond exchanging business cards and collecting LinkedIn connections. It is a philosophy—a way of building meaningful, purpose-driven relationships that honor the humanity in every individual. At its heart, this approach rests upon three timeless values that define how we engage with others in our professional and personal spheres:

1. Authenticity: Be Real. Be You.

Authenticity is the cornerstone of all genuine human connection. In a world filled with noise, pretense, and superficial interactions, showing up as your true self is a bold and refreshing act. It means presenting yourself honestly—your values, your story, your intentions—without the mask of who you think others expect you to be.

Authenticity fosters trust. When you are real, others feel safe to be real too. This mutual openness forms the bedrock of long-lasting relationships. Whether you're speaking at an event, meeting a potential client, or catching up with a colleague, let your words and actions be an extension of your truth. People may forget what you said, but they'll never forget how authentically you showed up.

2. Generosity: Share before You Seek

In human-centric networking, generosity is expressed most powerfully through the simple yet profound act of sharing—sharing your knowledge, your experience, your time, and your network. Rather than approaching relationships with the mindset of "What can I gain?", instead think about "What can I share that might help someone else?"

This approach transforms networking from a transactional activity into a meaningful exchange. It could be as small as sharing a piece of advice, recommending a helpful resource, introducing someone to a useful contact, or offering words of encouragement during a challenging time.

Sharing builds bridges. It creates a sense of trust, safety, and appreciation. More importantly, it invites others to do the same, fostering a culture of openness and mutual support.

When you share generously without expectations, you not only elevate others, but you also contribute to a richer, more connected professional ecosystem.

3. Intentionality: Build with Purpose

Intentionality means being deliberate about who you connect with, why you are building that relationship, and how you nurture it over time. It's about aligning your networking actions with your larger vision, values, and goals. Intentional networking fosters enduring connections that are mutually empowering. By comparison, random, scattered networking may only bring fleeting contacts.

Aim to invest time and energy in relationships that align with your values and where there's potential for mutual growth. Choose quality over quantity! Whether you're reaching out to a mentor, a peer, or a new contact, do it with thoughtfulness, clarity, and respect. Intentionality will help you to slow down and create relationships that matter.

The 3C Model of Human-Centric Networking: Connect. Contribute. Cultivate.

Three values—Authenticity, Generosity, and Intentionality—form the foundation of what I call the 3C Model of Human-Centric Networking. It brings these values to life through practical action.

1. CONNECT: Meaningful first impressions

A real connection begins the moment you show up—not just physically, but emotionally and mentally—with sincerity.

I recall attending my first business networking event nearly ten years ago. Nervous and unsure of what to say, I held my coffee close, as though its warmth could shield me from the discomfort of the unfamiliar. Then someone approached me with a simple question, "How can I help you?" That single question, offered with genuine warmth, shifted everything. He wasn't trying to pitch or impress. He was present, open, and kind. And that kindness opened the door to a connection grounded in generosity and trust.

Connection grows when:
- **You approach with purpose**

Instead of entering a room with the mindset of "What can I get?", ask yourself, "What can I learn?" or "Whom can I uplift today?" Purposeful presence means treating every encounter as a potential beginning of a meaningful relationship, not as a transaction. Ditch the elevator pitch for eye contact. Replace the sales script with a sincere smile. Show that you're more interested in people than in promotion.

- **You share with openness**

Let your guard down. You don't have to overshare, but a touch of vulnerability—sharing why you're passionate about your work, a personal story, or even a challenge you're navigating—can humanize you. This openness invites others to be more themselves too. *Realness is magnetic.*

- **You're present**

Listening is one of the most underrated networking skills. Be fully there. Put the phone away. Maintain eye contact. Nod, smile, and listen without interrupting. Reflect back what you heard with phrases like "That's interesting; tell me more," or "I hear you, and that reminds me..." *Presence is the language of respect.*

At your next event, whether in person or virtual, try this: start a conversation by being genuinely curious. Ask open-ended questions. Share something real about yourself. Let your warmth lead.

2. CONTRIBUTE: Give without keeping score

Once a connection forms, the question becomes: What can you offer?

Contribution doesn't always mean making introductions or offering business leads. Sometimes, the most valuable gifts are your time, encouragement, or insight. The magic happens when you give without expecting something in return.

Think about the trees in the forest. Beneath the trees lies a network called mycelium—a living web of fungal filaments that allows trees to share nutrients, send alerts, and support one another. The strongest trees feed the weaker ones so the whole forest thrives.

That's what a great network does. It shares, supports, and strengthens from within.

You can contribute by:

- **Sharing knowledge**

Did you read an article that made you think of someone's challenge or goal? Send it with a short note. Share your own lessons learned. Write posts that offer value to your network, not just self-promotion. When you give insight freely, you become a go-to person—not just for answers, but for inspiration.

- **Celebrating others**

Public recognition builds private bonds. When someone in your network achieves something—big or small—acknowledge it. A congratulatory comment on LinkedIn, a shout-out in a group, or a personal message of appreciation can uplift and motivate. Celebrating others shows you're not just watching—you're cheering.

- **Making introductions**

Be a bridge. When you see two people who could help each other, introduce them. Offer a few lines about each person to make the intro warm and thoughtful. Great networkers are connectors, and great connectors are remembered.

- **Being consistent**

Don't vanish after the first conversation. Stay visible through regular, meaningful engagement. Like and comment on posts. Send a message to check in. Share relevant opportunities. Consistency builds comfort—and comfort builds connection.

- **Offering your time**

Sometimes the best gift is your attention. Offer to hop on a call to brainstorm, mentor someone who's just starting out, or volunteer your skills for a cause that matters. Time is a precious currency—and when shared wisely, it yields exponential returns.

Contribution has a ripple effect. The more you give, the more trust and goodwill you create. The more trust you build, the more likely people are to think of you when opportunity knocks.

3. CULTIVATE: Nurture for the Long Term

Many professionals make great first impressions but then vanish. Follow-up fades— and with it, the potential of a powerful relationship.

Human-centric networking stands apart because it sees relationships as living, not fixed. Like a plant, a relationship needs water, light, and care. Cultivation isn't just polite follow-up. It's consistent, thoughtful engagement that says, "I value you, not just what you can do for me."

"Connection is the spark. Contribution is the fuel. But Cultivation is what keeps the fire burning." — *Yabeejan Koya*

Ways to Cultivate Include:
- **Follow up thoughtfully**

After a meeting, send a message or voice note to thank them for their time. Mention a specific insight from the conversation to show you were truly listening. Share a resource that can help them. Timely and relevant follow-up builds relational capital.

- **Stay personal**

Keep track of birthdays, anniversaries, and professional milestones. Drop a note during festive seasons or when you see something that reminds you of them. A simple "Thinking of you" message can rekindle dormant connections.

- **Be top of mind**

Regularly share updates about your work, lessons you've learned, or causes you care about. This keeps you visible without being pushy. Invite people to collaborate or co-create. Reach out when you find synergies in your networks. Show that you're not just waiting for the next favor—you're investing in mutual growth.

- **Reinvest in reciprocity**

A healthy network is not one-sided. If someone supports you, find a way to support them back—not out of obligation, but appreciation.

Reciprocity doesn't mean keeping score. It means staying aware of the ecosystem and feeding it with gratitude.

- **Create opportunities for reconnection**

Host small meetups. Arrange catch-up calls. Send out a monthly update or newsletter to your close network. These gentle touchpoints nurture new connections and can also reawaken dormant relationships.

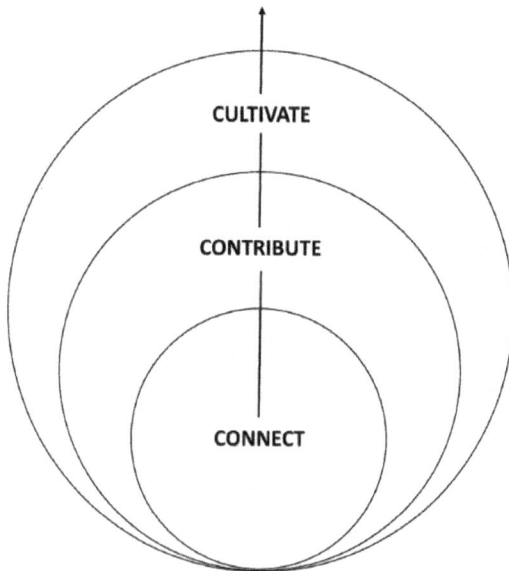

Think like a gardener: some seeds take months to sprout. Others may bloom unexpectedly after years. But if you keep showing up, watering with care, and removing weeds of neglect, you'll eventually walk through a garden of relationships richer than you ever imagined.

The 3C Model of Human-Centric Networking invites us to show up not just with our business cards, but with our hearts. It reminds us that relationships thrive on sincerity, not strategy.

When you Connect with intention, Contribute without expectation, and Cultivate with care, you don't just build a network—you build a legacy.

Let the 3C Model guide you. The world doesn't need more transactional networking. It needs human networking—where every connection becomes a chance to change lives, including your own.

The Payoff: Growth, Influence, and Opportunity

When done the human-centric way, networking delivers more than just leads. It creates ecosystems alive with potential, rich with trust, and ready to respond when you need support.

Human-centric networking helps you:

- Gain referrals and repeat business through trust-based relationships
- Attract speaking opportunities, collaborations, and media exposure
- Build a community that believes in your mission and amplifies your message

But perhaps most powerfully, it helps you feel less alone in business.

Because beyond strategy and success, we're all wired for connection. And when we feel truly seen, heard, and supported, our confidence grows. Our impact multiplies.

Practices to make networking human again

In a world chasing quick wins and digital reach, choosing to connect the human way is a bold act. But it's also a timeless one. It reminds us that business is built not just on ideas, but on relationships. And relationships are built not on scripts, but on genuine connection.

Relationships are built not on scripts, but on genuine connection.

So, the next time you find yourself in a room full of strangers—pause. Breathe. Be yourself. Ask a real question. Listen with your whole self. And trust that the right relationships—those rich with value, empathy, and mutual respect—will unfold from there.

To breathe life into a human-centric networking mindset, consider embedding these five practices into your routine. They're simple yet soulful shifts that can transform your connections from transactional to transformational.

Set Monthly Connection Intentions

Choose 3–5 people to reconnect with each month. No agenda. Just presence.

We often wait for the "right time" to reach out. But intentionality beats spontaneity when it comes to nurturing a vibrant network. At the start of each month, choose a small handful of people—perhaps someone you admire from afar, a former colleague, or even an old client you genuinely liked.

Send a short message just to say: *"I was thinking of you. How are you doing?"*

No pitches, no requests. Just presence and genuine curiosity. You'll be amazed how many doors this soft tap opens.

Quarterly Co-Creation

Partner with someone on a webinar, article, or initiative every quarter.

One of the most human ways to deepen a connection is to create something together. Think beyond formal collaborations—this could be co-hosting a virtual meet, brainstorming ideas over a shared Google Doc, or inviting someone to co-author a thought piece on LinkedIn.

It doesn't have to be polished or perfect. It just has to be real. When we co-create, we share space, vision, and energy. And that often leads to long-term bonds that go far beyond a single project.

Keep a 'Give List'

Jot down ways you can support your network—introductions, shout-outs, ideas.

Generosity is the heartbeat of human-centric networking. Keep a running list—on paper, in your notes app, or even a spreadsheet—of how you can add value. Maybe someone's launching a podcast and needs guests. Maybe you know two people who should meet. Maybe someone's work moved you, and a public shout-out would make their day.

You don't need to wait until you're asked. When you give first, without keeping score, you activate trust—and trust travels.

Host Micro-Meetups or Virtual Circles

Facilitate small group conversations where deeper dialogue can happen.

Big networking events can be noisy and overwhelming. Instead, host a 60-minute virtual circle or coffee meet-up with 4–6 people who might enjoy knowing each other. Create a theme—like "Leadership Lessons from Business Failures" or "What's Lighting You Up

This Month?"—to anchor the conversation.

When people feel seen and heard, they show up differently. You don't need to be an expert—just a host who makes space for real talk.

Reflect Regularly

After networking events, journal: What felt good? What felt forced? What would I do differently?

We often rush from one event to the next, without pausing to learn from our interactions. Take 10 minutes post-event to reflect. Did you feel energized or drained? Did a particular conversation light you up? Was there a moment when you didn't feel like yourself?

This gentle self-inquiry builds awareness, so you can start designing networking experiences that align with your values—not just your calendar.

Closing Reflection

Think of someone in your network who's made a real difference in your life or work. Have you told them?

Now think of someone you could support, encourage, or connect with today. What's one small gesture you can make?

Because your next big opportunity isn't in a stack of business cards. It's hidden in the genuine and generous human relationships you choose to build—one conversation at a time.

Yabeejan

About Yabeejan Koya

Yabeejan is a seasoned Business and Leadership Coach, Connection Catalyst, and Professional Speaker with over a decade of experience empowering business leaders, entrepreneurs and organisations to thrive through purposeful leadership, collaborative teamwork, and meaningful networking.

As Founder Partner of Infinito Business Services, he has facilitated training and coaching sessions, impacting more than 10,000 individuals across diverse industries. His strong foundation in business psychology, behavioural understanding, and applied learning allows him to design experiences that foster clarity, connection, and courageous action.

Yabeejan holds qualifications in Commerce, Entrepreneurship, and Applied Psychology, and brings rich cross-sectoral experience, including roles in global and national organisations. His ability to recognise and celebrate individual potential enables him to craft personalised growth journeys for individuals and teams.

He actively contributes as a leader and mentor in respected platforms like Business Network International (BNI), Junior Chamber International (JCI), Toastmasters International, and the Professional Speakers Association of India (PSAI).

Known for his calm presence, clarity of thought, and people-first approach, Yabeejan inspires others to lead authentically, build strong relationships, and create meaningful impact in their personal and professional spheres.

www.linkedin.com/in/yabeejan

Introducing Julie Nottage, New Zealand

Our next speaker knows that winning contracts isn't just about what you offer, it's about how confidently you connect. Julie Nottage is a Certified Speaking Professional and Chartered Engineer who brings both precision and presence to the stage. She has helped countless professionals transform their communication, build trust, and turn conversations into business opportunities. Today, Julie will share how confident networking - through storytelling, emotional intelligence, and purposeful communication - can move you from transactional meetings to meaningful relationships that win contracts. Please join me in welcoming a leader in confident communication and impactful leadership, Julie Nottage!

CHAPTER SIXTEEN
Confident Networking

*Building Relationships
That Last*

---

*"You can't build meaningful relationships on shaky
foundations. Connection starts from within."*

Many professionals shy away from networking because it feels awkward, unclear, or overly transactional. But great networking isn't about having the perfect pitch. It's about listening, asking meaningful questions, and knowing how to start and carry on conversations that build trust.

Drawing from my background in engineering, public speaking, and leadership, I'd like to offer anyone who feels shy about networking a structured yet human-centered approach to developing confidence. You'll learn how to overcome social anxiety, build rapport, guide conversations, and follow up with impact—online and in person.

Let's explore the emotional foundations of confident networking by unpacking the role of social anxiety, self-doubt, and the discomfort that often comes with connection. Many of us hesitate to engage, not because we lack skill but because of fear. Whether it's the fear of being judged, the presence of a confidence gap, or the tension raised when stepping outside our comfort zones, these inner barriers can block external opportunities. But we can reframe those fears as part of the growth process, use tools to manage anxiety, build self-awareness, and begin networking with confidence, not dread.

Confidence doesn't come first. Action does. And connection begins when we're brave enough to lean into the discomfort.

The fear of networking

Networking often brings up fear—fear of being judged, saying the wrong thing, or feeling out of place. Social anxiety is more common than most people realize. It can stop us from entering conversations or showing up at events. Understanding that this fear is natural is the first step to overcoming it. The goal isn't to eliminate fear but to learn how to manage it and build connection anyway.

Confidence and capability don't always go hand in hand. The "confidence gap" is what holds many skilled professionals back from stepping into opportunities. This gap forms due to internalized doubt, lack of feedback, or underrepresentation. The good news is that confidence can be built—and the first brick is self-awareness. When you see your own value and name the fears that hold you back, you lay the foundation for confidence to rise.

Discomfort when stretching your comfort zone is often seen as a warning to retreat, but it can be a guidepost toward growth. When you lean into discomfort, you uncover resilience, insight, and confidence that wasn't visible from your comfort zone. Networking becomes not something to fear but something to explore.

It's normal to feel a little hesitant before introducing yourself, especially in a networking setting. But that moment of uncertainty can be shifted into presence, and presence builds confidence. Open posture, steady eye contact, and calm gestures communicate confidence, even if you're feeling unsure inside. Body language is a powerful tool that can build rapport because people respond more to what they sense than what they hear. A confident stance signals self-trust, which encourages others to trust you. You don't need to feel confident to look confident—and that look can carry you until your mindset catches up.

Before any words are exchanged, we often connect through something simple: the handshake. A handshake is more than just a greeting; it's a moment to share goodwill. A firm, respectful handshake can set the tone for mutual respect. It's a silent agreement: I see you, and I stand present. Practice your handshake to reflect clarity and confidence without force or stiffness. Let your first impression speak well of you.

Confidence is more than just posture; it's presence. The way you walk into a room, the tone you use to greet someone, and the pace of your speech all send messages. Walk with purpose. Walk like you belong there, even if your nerves are saying otherwise. When you embody confidence physically, you activate it mentally. Eventually, how you act becomes how you feel.

Finding Your Voice

Your voice carries more than just your message; it carries your energy. People hear your nerves before they hear your words. Speaking with presence means grounding yourself before you speak. Slow down. Breathe. Project from your diaphragm, not your throat. Use the "pause with purpose" strategy: use pauses to show control and pause before making a key point. Practice speaking aloud. Your voice is one of your most underused assets. Strengthen it, and it becomes your amplifier in any room.

Tone, pace, and clarity influence how people perceive your confidence. A calm voice eases tension. Clear articulation and enunciation makes your message more accessible. And a steady pace keeps your listener engaged. Notice vocal habits like trailing off or speeding up. Your voice should reflect your message, not rush past it. When your tone aligns with your intent, your credibility rises.

Redesigning your introduction for impact

The old "Hi, I'm [name] and I'm a [job title]" just doesn't cut it anymore. People remember stories, not stats. Try introducing yourself with a purpose-led opener: "I help [people] achieve [benefit]." Lead with what you solve, not just your role. Your introduction is your headline. It should catch attention, communicate value, and leave a reason to follow up. Practice yours until it feels authentic and impactful.

Structured Conversations - From Rapport to Relationships

Successful networking isn't about "winging it." It's planned, structured, and directed with emotional intelligence and purpose."

Whether it's your first introduction or a follow-up call months later, remember that it's quality, not quantity. It's about saying what matters in a way that connects. Purposeful rapport-building, strategic storytelling, and emotional awareness are the conversational tools that can turn interactions into opportunities, and relationships into trusted networks.

In my home country of New Zealand, we value uplifting others through care, respect, and hospitality. This is steeped in our Māori traditions and culture. We even have a name for this: manaakitanga.

When applied to networking, it means approaching every interaction with generosity—listening deeply, offering help without expectation, and ensuring people feel seen and valued. Rapport isn't just about chemistry. It's about how we make others feel.

The 80/20 rapport rule

Rapport is built when you find the right blend of professional purpose and personal connection. The 80/20 rapport rule suggests 80% of your initial interaction can be professional and goal-oriented, while 20% should offer a glimpse of personality or shared human experience. This combination helps build trust without crossing boundaries. Don't overshare. Say just enough to make the other person feel like they're speaking with a real human, not a role or title.

People are more likely to trust you when they see something of themselves in you. Whether it's shared values, a hometown, an experience, or a mutual connection, finding common ground is a fast track to trust. Good networkers listen for clues and use them to spark connection. You don't need a long list of similarities; one shared idea can turn a conversation into a relationship.

Creating a circle of trust

Instead of striving to meet *more* people, focus on meaning more to the *right* people. Networking is a garden, not a vending machine. Relationships need tending, not just introductions. Follow up, check in, and offer support without asking for anything. Over time, this builds a circle of trust, a network of people who advocate for you, refer you, and open doors because they know who you are, not just what you do.

"Great communicators don't bulldoze. They navigate. They listen. They pivot with intention, holding space and guiding gently."

Listen first: Empathy as a strategic tool

When networking, don't aim to be interesting. Be interested. Strategic empathy is your most powerful tool. It means fully listening, not just to the words, but to the energy behind them. When someone feels genuinely heard, they're far more likely to remember you, trust you, and want to connect again. We do business with people we know, like, and trust. Great networkers don't jump in with their elevator pitch at the first pause. They reflect the speaker's language, ask thoughtful follow-up questions, and notice cues like tone, pace, and body language.

Facts tell. Emotion sells. Many of us rely too much on facts and achievements, forgetting that emotions create connection. Speak from your why, not just your what. Instead of listing features or credentials, share the impact. Help people feel something, and they'll remember you long after the networking event ends. Avoid info dumps and start with impact.

Story invites trust, but so does direction. A confident speaker can guide the conversation without overpowering it.

Emotional intelligence means knowing what's appropriate—and when. Networking isn't a therapy session, but it also shouldn't be robotic. Choose stories and insights that are timely, relevant, and respectful of the other person's context. If in doubt, keep it light, and observe. Emotional Intelligence (EQ) helps you read the room, match their energy, and know what's appropriate. Use EQ as your compass to guide what you say and how you say it.

Sometimes a conversation drifts, and that's okay. But skilled networkers know how to gently steer it back to a meaningful or relevant topic. The "Twisting Technique" allows you to link something they've said to something you care about. For example, "That reminds me of a project we're working on…" It's polite, it's subtle, and it works. It shows you're engaged—and it creates a bridge to share your value.

But effective networkers know how to gently steer small talk toward something more meaningful. A simple conversational structure can help build rapport while naturally uncovering professional alignment. Start by showing genuine curiosity about why someone's there, what they're working on, and how you might be able to support or connect them further. This creates value on both sides, without forcing the conversation.

The Evolution of Connection – From Handshakes to Hyperlinks

Networking is no longer bound by in-person events or handshakes. It's become borderless. You can build genuine professional relationships across cities, time zones, and industries with the click of a button. But in this global context, the principles of presence and intention matter more than ever. Whether you're on Zoom, LinkedIn, or Teams, people notice how you show up, digitally and energetically.

While we may not always be in the same room, the essence of face-to-face connection still matters. You can meet someone over Zoom, spark a conversation in a LinkedIn comment, or build rapport through a thoughtful voice note or email. The platforms have changed, but the purpose hasn't. People still want to feel seen, heard, and valued.

The most effective networkers today are those who can create real connection across screens and time zones, using small moments to make a lasting impact. So let's explore how to bring authenticity, presence, and connection into digital networking spaces—whether you're in a virtual breakout room, following up after a webinar, or reaching out to someone across the world. It's about showing up with the same mana, warmth, and intention online as you would in person.

It might be a quick "thanks for sharing" comment, a thoughtful emoji reaction, or a private follow-up to a public post. These micro-moments might seem small, but they accumulate. Each one says, "I see you." Use the tools available—reactions, comments, chat boxes—to stay visible in meaningful ways.

Your virtual presence matters. A poor camera angle or a low-energy voice can erode the professionalism you intend to show. Position yourself well. Speak clearly. Show up with warmth. People can sense presence, even through a screen. Show them your professionalism and personality in equal measure. Don't just log on. Show up and stand out.

Know before you go: Plan with purpose

Great networkers don't leave connections to chance. They plan with purpose. Before you step into any networking event, webinar, or meeting (in-person or online), take time to research who'll be there. Who do you want to meet? Why? What value can you offer them, and what might you learn in return? Have a few conversation starters ready, know your key messages, and go in with curiosity. When you show up informed and engaged, people notice and will remember you for all the right reasons.

Julie

About Julie Nottage

Julie Nottage is a Certified Speaking Professional and Chartered Engineer who transforms corporate teams into confident communicators and impactful leaders. Blending her engineering precision with powerful presence and persuasive communication, she helps professionals speak with clarity, overcome self-doubt, and lead boldly. Julie is passionate about unlocking stronger leadership, deeper connection, and high performance—ultimately driving business growth and revenue in today's competitive world.

www.julienottage.com

For Networking with Purpose

1. Check your camera, lighting, and posture before every online call. Presence is still powerful, even on screen.

2. Comment meaningfully on three people's posts this week. It keeps you visible and valuable.

3. Reach out to someone in a different region or industry this month. Build a borderless network.

4. Plan a few open-ended, driven questions that feel natural to you: "What brought you here?" → "What are you working on?" → "How can I support that?"

5. If they mention a challenge, don't launch into a solution. Pause and say, "That sounds tricky. How are you handling it?" That moment of empathy builds trust faster than any sales pitch.

6. Next time you're in a networking conversation, focus on listening without the pressure to impress. Use prompts like: "That's really interesting. What led you to that?" or "I'd love to hear more about that project."

7. Craft a 60-second story about a moment you helped solve a problem, and practice telling it aloud.

8. Ask, "What got you into your field?" to uncover shared values or experiences.

9. Use the "pause with purpose" method: slow your speech and pause before your key points and at the end of your key points.

10. Rewrite your introduction using this format: "I help [who] achieve [what benefit] through [your solution]."

11. Practice your posture in front of a mirror. Stand tall, grounded, and relaxed — even when you're unsure.

12. Walk with purpose. Walk into your next meeting with slow, purposeful steps and a quiet inner mantra: "I belong here."

13. Record yourself introducing yourself or giving a presentation. Listen back to your tone, pace, and clarity. How many um's and er's?

14. Growth lives on the edge of discomfort. Say yes to one small opportunity that stretches you.

15. Confidence is built through action. Reflect weekly on one situation where you stepped outside your comfort zone.

16. Write down two questions you can ask someone at your next event. Ask the questions to shift the focus off yourself and onto others.

We hope you have enjoyed reading this book and have been inspired by the many exceptional speakers and authors featured here.

The **Virtual Speakers Association International** is a supporting organization offering networking, development and events for people around the world who are professional speakers, trainers and facilitators of learning. If you would like to learn more about us and how we may be able to support your journey as a professional speaker, or if you would like to engage with any of our speakers for your next event any where in the world, please visit us today at:

www.vsainternational.org

Want More?
Your conference doesn't end here - we've got more to share.

Maybe you're interested in being part of one of our *next books* in this series or *sponsorship opportunities*?

What about turning your next industry conference into a **CONFERENCE IN A BOOK**™ *special edition*?

Scan the **QR code** or visit
www.indieexpertspublishing.com/conferenceinabook

- › Get exclusive bonus resources (*Access Password:* ***CIAB#125***)
- › Be the first to know about upcoming volumes in the series
- › Access tools, guides, and insights you won't find anywhere else

Stay connected. Keep learning. Keep leading.

Conference in a Book™

Proudly brought to you by Indie Experts Publishing

www.ingramcontent.com/pod-product-compliance
Lightning Source LLC
Chambersburg PA
CBHW040754220326
41597CB00029BA/4786